P9-CDW-077

Political Succession in the USSR

Political Succession in the USSR

by MYRON RUSH

COLUMBIA UNIVERSITY PRESS
New York and London 1965

Myron Rush is a Soviet specialist with The RAND Corporation and is currently Visiting Professor of Government at Cornell University. This book is a publication of The RAND Corporation and of the Research Institute on Communist Affairs of Columbia University.

Library of Congress Catalogue Card Number: 65–14778
Manufactured in the United States of America

To my father and son Victor

Acknowledgments

I am indebted to The RAND Corporation and the Research Institute on Communist Affairs, Columbia University, for their support and encouragement. Professor Philip E. Mosely of Columbia University provided a detailed and comprehensive critique of an early draft that proved valuable in my further work on the book. My colleagues at different times and places, Allan Bloom, Zbigniew Brzezinski, Herbert Dinerstein, Arnold Horelick, and Thomas Wolfe, commented helpfully at various stages. I am indebted to Lilita Dzirkals for competent research assistance throughout. I remain responsible, of course, for the book's accuracy, argument, and conclusions.

My work on this book was done at three different institutions at opposite ends of the country. To my wife, who bore up with good cheer in moving between these various places of residence and in living in them, I am grateful.

Myron Rush

Ithaca, New York
November, 1964

Contents

Introduction

This manuscript was completed prior to the coup d'état which deprived Khrushchev of his position as ruler, and thus precipitated the inevitable succession crisis that the Soviet Union is now undergoing. The author has been studying and writing about succession in the USSR for several years in the conviction that the lack of legitimate and recognized means for the transfer of power is the crucial problem within the Soviet regime, and that there is a qualitative difference between Soviet politics in a period of personal rule and Soviet politics in a period of succession. Under a personal ruler the principal problem is formulating policy and gaining acceptance for it; in a period of succession the principal problem is determination of who in fact, if not in right, can make the decisions.

The purpose of the present study is to present a theoretical analysis and historical account of the problem of succession in the USSR, to lay bare Khrushchev's arrangements for the transfer of power, and to provide guidelines for understanding developments in the Khrushchev succession. I have outlined the strategies and institutions which can be used by the contestants for power and considered possible effects of the struggle on the regime. Moreover, because a proper understanding of Soviet succession is crucial in the formulation of U.S. policy, I have tried to indicate briefly the bearing of the Khrushchev succession on foreign affairs.

Khrushchev, to my surprise, failed to preserve the power he had concentrated, perhaps because his overconfidence enabled his intended successors to acquire too much power. Fundamentally, however, his overthrow illustrates the double dilemma, here discussed at some length, of a ruler in the Soviet Union who attempts to govern without terror and to arrange for his own succession. The succession has begun in an unexpected but not overlooked way. It will now proceed, I believe, within the context of the possibilities and using the means this book defines. The effect of the Khrushchev succession on the regime will, if anything, be increased by the way in which it was initiated.

In the short interval between Khrushchev's overthrow and the book's publication, I introduced a substantial number of small changes in the manuscript, chiefly to save the reader the annoyance of reading about a past event as though it still lay in the future, but also to highlight the pitfalls in Khrushchev's attempt to arrange the succession. Khrushchev's overthrow itself is discussed briefly in an Epilogue.

Even before the onset of the Khrushchev succession, the prospect of it received considerable attention in the West. Unlike forecasts of the Stalin succession, however, it has been widely believed that the Khrushchev succession will not be highly consequential. There are several reasons for this relative depreciation.

Stalin's person amply filled the Soviet political scene when he ruled, and this was recognized by almost all qualified observers. On occasion, Presidents Truman and Eisenhower expressed the view that the true source of what was evil in Soviet foreign policy was to be sought not in Stalin but in the men around him, but this was certainly an aberration. Actually, Stalin so overshadowed his lieutenants that the West knew relatively little of their political character until after his death, and they may have been unsure of it themselves. With Khrushchev it is different. The extent of his power was disputed among Soviet specialists throughout the period following the removal of his chief opponents from the leadership in 1957. A large group of Western observers were convinced that Khrushchev was but a spokesman for a collective leadership. If his place in the leadership was so modest, however, vacating it seemed unlikely to produce great consequences.

There is another reason the significance of the Khrushchev succession has been depreciated. By the time Stalin died, he had brought rule by terror close to the limits of its possibilities. Despite his great accomplishments, changes were required to overcome the bureaucratic inertia and disaffection that were inevitable results of his system of rule. This was widely recognized in the West, and it was confirmed by the initial policies of his heirs. While they disagreed as to the character and extent of the changes required, they all accepted the need for radical change. In the decade since Stalin's death, his system of rule has been significantly altered, although not in the decisive respects. While many Western observers are disappointed that the Stalin succession did not lead to far greater and more beneficent changes in the Soviet political system, it is widely believed that the acute social and political problems that Stalin bequeathed to his heirs have been resolved. The Soviet political system has been stabilized, it is thought, and the Khrushchev succession is not likely to upset it.

In the realm of foreign policy, there has been a similar accommodation to the needs of the time. While Stalin continued to adhere to outmoded doctrines of the regime's early years, his heirs have come to terms with the Nuclear Age.

The elements of this argument contain much that is true, but the conclusion to which the argument leads may be in error. In this book an attempt will be made to establish the following assertions:

First, in the Soviet political system, the passing of the ruler inevitably produces a crisis in the leadership.

Second, since Khrushchev was the ruler, exercising decisive authority, the regime faces a serious problem in the Khrushchev succession.

Third, the changes in Soviet politics and in Soviet society effected by Stalin's heirs have produced an equilibrium, it is true, but it is an unstable equilibrium. It is a question whether Soviet society will preserve the basic features of its post-Stalin phase.

The order of inquiry is as follows.

First, the elements of political succession in general and their particular manifestations in some types of government will be discussed, not in a systematic treatise (although one is badly needed), but more or less aphoristically, to establish the character of the problem. We shall then present short accounts of the two succession crises the USSR has so far experienced, the first beginning in 1922, when Lenin fell ill, the second in 1953, when Stalin died suddenly. We shall not trace these events in detail but only their essentials, in order to draw instruction from them. We shall then present a theory of succession in the USSR, and finally inquire into the Khrushchev succession.

This is the order of our inquiry; a word must be said as to its character. As we shall argue, the succession is indeterminate. It poses a problem for the Soviet rulers, who cannot know whether they will solve it. The outside observer, being ignorant of much that is known to them, must be even more uncertain of the outcome. But though the succession is essentially unpredictable, it is subject to a necessity that is intelligible. Since succession is an event that will happen to the Soviet regime, its possibilities are limited by what the regime is. Relying on facts and well-founded suppositions, therefore, one may hope to advance by reasonable arguments to plausible conclusions. The object of this study of the Khrushchev succession is to identify the determinate elements that arise from the nature of the Soviet political system in its present state of development, while holding in view the essential indeterminacy of the succession.

Of all these Formes of Government, the matter being mortall, so that not onely Monarchs, but also whole Assemblies dy, it is necessary for the conservation of the peace of men, that as there was order taken for an Artificiall Man [the state], so there be order also taken for an Artificiall Eternity of life. . . . This Artificiall Eternity is that which men call the Right of Succession.

Hobbes, *Leviathan,* chapter XIX

I: Political Succession

Political succession is the transfer of sovereign power from a ruler or government to a successor. Such rotation is made inevitable by man's mortality, but it does not always wait on the death of leaders. Since changed circumstances cannot always be met by change in the leaders themselves, they may be required by the constitution or compelled by force to leave office during their own lifetime.

The current ruler's identity is always known, at least to the inner circle, but the identity of those who are to succeed may or may not be known in advance. Similarly, the time of transfer (or renewal) of power may be specified in advance, as in constitutional regimes, or may depend on the demise or incapacity of the ruler, which cannot be foreseen with certainty. The manner in which power is transferred may be prescribed and established firmly by custom and tradition, or it may be left indeterminate.

If the transfer of power is not accomplished at once, succession proceeds in fairly distinct phases. In the first phase, the preceding ruler's power is assumed by others so that government may continue; in the second, power is redistributed in more stable and lasting form; finally, there may be a third phase of consolidation. These distinct phases occur in hereditary monarchy when the new monarch is too young to rule and a regency is established. They may also occur in the succession to a personal dictator who has concentrated great power in his hands. When the dictator dies or is incapacitated, his lieutenants, having lived in his shadow, seldom are able to make good at once a personal claim to the plenitude of his power. It is usually divided and shared for a time, as in the triumvirate established after Julius Caesar's death. But if shared rule proves unstable, the regime will founder, or there may be a new concentration of power in a second phase of succession. Thus Augustus finally arrogated to himself the power Julius Caesar had usurped. Subsequently, he consolidated his vast power and made himself emperor.

The central question in political succession is that of legitimacy: By what right does the successor rule? The legitimacy of the successor may be brought in question in any regime, but this danger is especially acute where institutions have been newly established and are as yet unsupported by strong sentiment or habits of obedience. It is not simply a question of the legitimacy of the new regime. The founder's right to rule is acknowledged, at least by those who accept the regime he has established; but what of his political heirs? The questionable legitimacy of the Roman emperors who followed Augustus, and its consequences, has been well characterized by the historian M. Rostovtzeff:

> Such were the conditions under which the successors of Augustus rose to the throne. Not one of them was convinced of his right to rule; they all lived in the steadily waning light of the charm exercised by the founder of their line. Hence the chief anxiety of all the emperors in the first century is to secure their position; they all dread rivals whose right is equal or superior to their own. . . . All these emperors feared not only

their personal rivals but also the attempts of the Senate to reassert itself.[1]

Every revolution leaves as its legacy the questionable legitimacy of the ruler. The present age of revolutions has produced many insecure dictators, whose sometimes frenzied efforts to justify their rule have led them to manufacture a synthetic charisma at best, and at worst to the imposition of terrible blood purges. As we shall see, the Russian Revolution also left its heritage of questionable legitimacy. The men who followed Lenin have behaved not unlike Augustus' successors: they have feared not only one another, but also, though in less degree, the sovereign bodies established by the Soviet constitution and the party statute.

Legitimacy of succession is a problem faced by all regimes, and their continuance depends upon successfully providing for it. If the transfer of authority is accomplished only with great difficulty, succession produces a crisis, a turning point for the system of rule. The crisis may affect only the direction of policy, but if it goes deep enough, it may put in question political institutions, and may even end a system of rule. It played a role, though not a great one, in the fall of the tsarist regime in 1917, which was somewhat hastened by the refusal of Archduke Michael to assume the throne left vacant by the forced abdication of Nicholas II.

Ordering the succession involves several closely related problems. Adopting a simple solution for one may only accentuate the difficulty encountered with others. For example, by identifying the heir presumptive and establishing his right to rule, hereditary monarchy readily deter-

[1] M. Rostovtzeff, *Rome,* tr. by J. D. Duff (New York, Oxford University Press, 1960), p. 195.

mines who is meant to receive sovereign power; but the ruler so designated may be immature, weak, or foolish. This difficulty may be obviated if the ruler is allowed to choose his successor, as was done at times in the Roman Empire and in eighteenth-century Russia. But to name a successor is to confer on him means that he can use to challenge the sovereign. He therefore has an interest in putting off the naming of an heir, and even in encouraging contention among rivals for the succession as a means of securing his own power. If he delays too long, however, the continuing uncertainty regarding his choice of successor may so intensify the maneuvering of the various candidates as to create political disorder.

The place of succession in the politics of states varies. If the ruler has great power, like that of oriental despots or modern dictators, its transfer is likely to be difficult; but if he shares power with others in an oligarchy, or if he rules in a classical "republic" or a modern liberal democracy, the problem is appreciably eased.

The mode and circumstances of succession also naturally affect its difficulty. An able and vigorous king ruling over a secure and stable realm and possessed of healthy sons need only be concerned to educate them for the distant day when they are to rule after him. But the politics of a dictatorship in which the ruler is old or mortally ill may be dominated by maneuvering for the succession. In a well-ordered constitutional regime, the seriousness of succession is diminished, although the difficulties attending it may vary considerably according to the occasion that gives rise to it. If the head completes his term of office the transfer of power is usually accomplished easily, but it may be attended with some difficulty if he dies in office. There may be even greater difficulty if the head of government becomes incapacitated for his office, since it is hard to establish a safe procedure for determining such incapacity. If provision is made for these eventualities, as in the U.S. Constitution, where the Vice President exercises the powers of the President when he is unable to, much depends on how the heir presumptive is chosen and what functions he performs before succeeding to power. If he is given no role in government, the office may not attract able men. It can also result in great powers being thrust upon a leader who has not been readied for their exercise. But if his role in government is too active, he may become a rival to his chief. The conflicting requirements of preparing the future ruler for his functions and of protecting the current ruler from a powerful rival is not a peculiarity of constitutional regimes; it also poses an acute problem for personal dictators.

The circumstances in which succession occurs may greatly influence its course and outcome. Even in a constitutional regime, the occurrence of succession at a time of danger is a source of trouble. It was at such a time that the Civil War began in America. In a dictatorial regime the manner of the dictator's departure from the political scene may be a crucial circumstance. If he dies suddenly, the power struggle that follows may be concentrated and acute. On the other hand, if he goes slowly after prolonged illness, his final passing may be but another event in a crisis of succession that is already raging. During his illness members of his household may gain political importance by controlling access to his person. This is more likely to happen if they have previously participated in politics and have been associated with some of the contenders for succession.

The protracted illness of the ruler has posed special problems for the succession throughout history. A special problem of modern times is the increased incidence of aging leaders whose mental powers are on the decline. In part this is due to the political revolutions of our times.[2] Many patriots, after prolonged struggle for their country's independence, have at long last come to power in old age when the opponent has finally suffered defeat or grown tired of the struggle. Syngman Rhee in Korea, Gandhi in India, Kenyatta in Kenya, among others, all gained personal political power in this way in their later years. In states defeated in World War II the place of "the missing generation" of leaders, who either collaborated with tyranny or were crushed by it, was taken by an older generation. Adenauer in West Germany, Gasperi in Italy, and Hatoyama in Japan came in this way to head their respective governments. Adversity has sometimes compelled states that were poorly led finally to turn over the reins of government to those who had long demanded patriotic sacrifice rather than promising personal ease. In this way Churchill first became prime minister in Great Britain at sixty-six.

While there are political reasons why men of advanced years sometimes have been selected to lead, they have been available for reasons that are at least partly medical. The progress of medicine helped them to survive physically,

2 See Dankwart A. Rustow, "Succession in the Twentieth Century," in *Journal of International Affairs,* No. 1 (1964), pp. 104–13. This entire issue is on "statesmen and succession."

often after having led hard lives. Partly for the same reason, rulers in relatively stable and authoritarian regimes have been able to grow old in the exercise of power. Among them are dictators like Franco in Spain and Salazar in Portugal, as well as democratic leaders like Nehru, who ruled for over fifteen years until his death at seventy-four. Modern medicine has opened enticing prospects for ambitious leaders, particularly dictators, of extending their reign. Stalin, for one, encouraged medical research in the USSR to seek ways of prolonging the blessings of his rule. One effect of improved medical treatment for the ruler, however, may be to prolong his life when he is mortally ill, so that his authority, based on his office or past accomplishments, may outlast his ability.

As the diseases of old age are overcome, aged and aging leaders are likely to be more and more with us. But whether they will continue to occupy positions of supreme power will depend on political circumstances that cannot be foreseen. Younger generations, especially in the new states, feeling themselves less burdened with the experience of a past that is felt to be distasteful or irrelevant, may be unwilling to entrust their fate for long to men of advanced years and increasingly eager to exercise power themselves. The gradual succession of the aged will doubtless remain an important question among governments, yet it may be increasingly resolved by impatient thrusts from below.

The ruler may be removed by assassination, which ordinarily is a complicating factor in the succession. If assassination occurs in the palace, it may not be known for what it is, yet the successor's legitimacy will probably be clouded with suspicion. If assassination occurs in the streets, the ruler's heirs may take measures to ensure their own security which can weaken the state's. A sense of shock inevitably attends the assassination of the ruler, particularly when this occurs in a public place. If the institutions are not secure, they too may feel the shock, particularly if the ruler's violent end encourages foreign attack.

Whether brought on by age, political convulsion, or constitutional limitation, political succession is inevitable. The transfer of power is best coped with by means that the regime has incorporated through time and has proven in practice. The founder of a new political system, such as Lenin, has no such means at his disposal. He must establish the method of succession as he established the method of rule, and to arrange the succession is, if anything, the more difficult of the two. To found political institutions requires knowledge of what is needful for man at a particular time, as well as the means of interposing the founder's will in the particular conjunction of circumstances. But to perpetuate political institutions requires the founder to project his will upon circumstances that cannot be foreseen in their entirety.[3] Chance may interpose itself to thwart his purpose in two different ways: first, some unexpected development may significantly alter the circumstances; second, the founder's will may not be projected upon the circumstances in the manner he intended.

To be effective, a will must have at its disposal a living body. Once he is incapacitated or dead, a former ruler,

[3] See "The Limits of Politics: King Lear, Act I, scene 1," by Harry V. Jaffa, in *Shakespeare's Politics* by Allan Bloom with Harry V. Jaffa (New York, Basic Books, 1964), pp. 113–45.

like Hamlet's father, must depend on another to effect his purpose in the matter of succession. And his instrument may prove weak, like Hamlet, for the task at hand, or may prove to have a divergent will. To succeed in arranging the succession, the ruler needs good luck; he may easily fail through no fault of his own.

II: The Lenin Succession

The first Soviet confrontation with the problem of succession came with Lenin's passing from power.[1] Because it was the first, there was no fund of experience on which to rely. The principals were led to seek parallels in the French Revolution which actually exerted some influence on developments because no more relevant historical experience was available. The characteristic problem of the Lenin succession was the need to find some substitute for Lenin, who was perhaps the most remarkable political figure of the twentieth century. His mode of rule was hardly to be duplicated, since Lenin's immense power over his lieutenants flowed from their recognition of his political genius, and their awe before his great deeds, which had been crowned with almost unhoped-for successes. For Lenin, unlike those who were to come after him, power derived from personal authority. Nevertheless, the Lenin

[1] There is a large literature on the Lenin succession, of which the following are notable: E. H. Carr, *A History of Soviet Russia* (New York, Macmillan, 1951–1960); Robert V. Daniels, *The Conscience of the Revolution* (Cambridge, Harvard University Press, 1960); I. Deutscher, *The Prophet Unarmed: Trotsky, 1921–1929* (London, Oxford University Press, 1959); A. Erlich, *The Soviet Industrialization Debate, 1924–1928* (Cambridge, Harvard University Press, 1960); B. Souvarine, *Stalin* (New York, Alliance Book Corporation, 1939).

succession proved to be the pattern from which the Stalin succession was largely shaped, even though Stalin's political character and mode of rule were radically different from Lenin's.

Even apart from its historical and potential effects on subsequent instances of succession in the USSR, the Lenin succession was crucial for the nascent regime. Since Lenin was the founder of the Bolshevik Party and of the Soviet state, his passing from power was bound to raise the question whether his successors would be able to preserve these political institutions. There was a still larger problem implicit in his succession, since Party and state existed only to further the Revolution. Could Lenin's successors realize the aims of the Revolution, the achievement of Socialism and then Communism?

The initial phase of the Lenin succession began May 26, 1922, when Lenin had his first stroke. During the preceding six months he had already been forced to reduce his political activities, but he still was able to dominate the XI Party Congress (April, 1922). His stroke the following month ended his career as the supreme authority in Russia, and made him instead the central figure in the struggle for succession.

In one sense the timing of the succession was unfortunate for the Bolsheviks. The sharing of Lenin's power began when he was only fifty-two years old, within five years of the October Revolution and less than two years after the ending of civil and foreign war. The circumstances of succession, however, favored Lenin's efforts to influence its course and outcome. He did not die suddenly, before the problem was upon him. For over nine months, until

March, 1923, he had the use of his weakened but still remarkable faculties of thought and expression. Possessing an overriding will to power, Lenin doubtless found it difficult to reconcile himself to surrendering the power he had sought for a quarter of a century and had but so recently acquired. He hoped for a complete recovery so that he could resume his search for the road to Socialism. Yet his awareness that he might not recover gave him time both to reflect upon the problem of succession and to act upon his reflections. While he was confined to his country residence much of the time between May, 1922, and March, 1923, he was able to rely upon his wife and political companion, Krupskaya, and on politically experienced secretaries to provide him with information and to communicate his wishes.

Lenin understood the need to act. Despite his modest manner, he knew his worth. In order not to deprive the Revolution of its leader, he had generally avoided personal danger, even going so far as to remain in hiding in the days before the Bolshevik uprising. He was aware, in 1922, that his political demise would bring on a crisis of the Revolution.

Lenin possessed exceptional means for influencing the succession. As the maker of the Revolution, his will on major questions was decisive. He had been right and his lieutenants wrong on so many crucial matters, that many of them were in awe of his political instincts and astuteness. On the few occasions after 1917 when Lenin's will was strongly resisted, his threat to resign carried the day. Lenin thus possessed at once: an understanding of the need to arrange the succession; the most suitable means for the purpose—a kind of personal authority that does not depend upon physical compulsion; and the opportunity to employ these means to best advantage.

On the whole, Lenin made good use of this favorable conjuncture. His efforts to arrange the succession, while far from faultless, display the political faculties that made him the most remarkable political figure of his time. Yet, as we shall see, he failed. Lenin's failure was due in part, perhaps, to bad fortune, but what is more significant, it reflects the limits of politics.[2]

At the time of Lenin's first stroke, the Bolshevik regime had gained a certain stability. Domestic opponents had been defeated by arms, the New Economic Policy had helped restore the economy after War Communism, and the American Relief Administration had helped to ameliorate the famine after the terrible draught of 1921. The Party's power over the country was becoming concentrated in its "apparatus" of full-time Party workers, and control of this apparatus was increasingly centralized in the Central Committee's Secretariat in Moscow.

In his rule, Lenin relied on the government, which he headed as Chairman of the Council of People's Commissars, as well as the Party apparatus, which was subject to him as the acknowledged leader of the Party, although he had no office in it. His chief aides were the following: in the government, the Deputy Chairman, Alexei Rykov; in the Party apparatus, Stalin, who as General Secretary of the Central Committee was its formal head; Leon Trotsky, War Commissar; and Georgi Zinoviev, head of the Comintern. The chief deliberative body in the formation of policy was the seven-man Politburo (Lenin, Trot-

[2] See the essay of that title by Harry V. Jaffa in *Shakespeare's Politics* by Allan Bloom (New York, Basic Books, 1964), pp. 113–45.

sky, Stalin, Zinoviev, Kamenev, Rykov, and Tomsky), but the Secretariat was supplanting the Council of People's Commissariats as the chief executive agency of rule.

In the earliest phase of succession, between Lenin's first and second strokes (May-December, 1922), his absence from the leadership, and later his reduced participation in it, substantially altered the political situation. Trotsky, whose prestige in the Party was second only to Lenin's, was widely feared in the top leadership as a potential Bonaparte, that is, as a creature of the Revolution who might become its subverter. Deprived of Lenin's personal support, Trotsky gradually was isolated within the top leadership. He became virtually a second-class member of the Politburo, along with the two new members, Rykov and Tomsky, who were raised to the Politburo in April, 1922, just before Lenin fell ill. The three remaining members of the seven-man Politburo, Zinoviev, Kamenev, and Stalin, began to form themselves into a troika, or ruling triumvirate. As we shall see, Stalin, in particular, was able to benefit in the first phase of Lenin's illness.

Consolidation of this triumvirate was interrupted by Lenin's renewed activity in the fall of 1922, but since the grouping had a natural basis in fear of Trotsky, the interruption was to prove only temporary.

Lenin, on his return to activity around September, 1922, found it difficult to recover his old grip on affairs. There were things to disapprove of, and his disapproval no longer sufficed to put an end to them. This was partly the consequence of an appointment that had been made shortly before Lenin's first stroke. The full effects of Stalin's "election" to the newly created post of General Secretary of the

Central Committee did not become known to Lenin until his return to affairs. In late December, nine months after the appointment, Lenin reported his discovery that "Comrade Stalin, having become general secretary, has concentrated enormous power in his hands." [3] Some of this "enormous power" had been Lenin's before his illness. A Lenin possessed of his full faculties no doubt could have reversed this development. But by the time of his remark about Stalin's newly acquired power, Lenin had already suffered his second stroke, on December 16, 1922. From this date forward, Lenin never appeared in public, and, what is more important, he rarely, if ever, saw his former subordinates in the top leadership, and had to communicate with them in writing.[4]

The next phase of the succession, between the second and third strokes (December 16, 1922, and March 9, 1923), was the period in which Lenin attempted to interpose his will upon the succession. While confined to his apartment, he was still able to think clearly and, with the aid of his secretaries, to set his thoughts down in writing. We shall treat this phase in some detail since it bears closely on our theme, and unusually revealing documentary materials are available. But the intrinsic difficulty of the political task attempted by the failing genius of Lenin, the psychological interest in the developing antagonism of the two titans, Lenin and Stalin, the decisive character of the outcome

[3] "Unpublished Documents of V. I. Lenin," note dictated December 24, 1922, *Kommunist,* No. 9 (June, 1956), p. 17.

[4] E. H. Carr, *The Interregnum* (New York, Macmillan, 1954), pp. 257–58. According to Trotsky, however, Stalin asserted in late February, 1923, "that Lenin had suddenly called him in and had asked him for poison." *Stalin* (New York, Harpers, 1941), p. 376.

and the great human tragedy that it entailed, these are large themes that still remain to be recorded adequately for the instruction of men.

A week after his second stroke, Lenin began to dictate a series of notes. Within a month there were thirteen of them, all bearing, directly or indirectly, on the problem of succession and on the means for advancing towards Socialism in Lenin's absence. Among them was "a letter to the Congress" of the Party that came to be known as "Lenin's testament," the parts of which were dictated on December 23, 24, and 25, and on January 4, 1923.

In the first note (dated December 23) Lenin directed himself to the problem of succession, though without explicit reference to his own failing health. He spoke of the "great danger [to which] our Central Committee would be exposed in case future developments would not be favorable to us," and of the need to prevent "conflicts between small Central Committee groupings which would gravely affect the fate of the Party as a whole." His solution was dispersal of authority, by raising the authority of the Central Committee and enlarging its membership from twenty-seven to as many as fifty or a hundred.[5]

The following day, when Lenin resumed dictation he amplified his remarks on the danger that he sought to avert, namely, "a split in the Party."[6] Throughout this letter to the Congress, Lenin's preoccupation with the question of personalities is evident. He does acknowledge that no measures could bring about the stability of the Central Committee if the two classes on whom the Party

[5] *Kommunist,* No. 9 (June, 1956), pp. 16–17.
[6] *Ibid.,* pp. 17–18.

rested (the working class and the peasantry) failed to "reach agreement." However, this was a long-term danger.[7]

LENIN'S SUCCESSORS

In Lenin's view, the immediate danger arose from the personal and political qualities of individual leaders who might succeed to his power:

> I have in mind stability as a guarantee against a split in the near future and I intend to examine here a series of considerations of a purely personal nature.

In his note of the previous day he had referred in general terms to the need for preventing "conflicts between small C.C. groupings." Now he specified the source of his concern: the conflict between Stalin and Trotsky. Lenin broods over this problem throughout the letter to the Congress, making it his central concern:

> I think that what is fundamental in the matter of stability—from this point of view—is such members of the Central Committee as Stalin and Trotsky. The relation between them constitutes, in my opinion, a big half of the danger of that split which might be avoided. . . .
>
> Comrade Stalin, having become General Secretary, has concentrated enormous power in his hands and I am not at all certain that he is capable of always utilizing this power with sufficient caution. Comrade Trotsky, on the other hand, as was already demonstrated in his fight against the Central Committee in connection with the question of the People's Commissariat of Communications, is distinguished not only by his remarkable abilities—personally he is, to be sure, the most able

[7] Actually what Lenin, as a Marxist, believed to be chiefly a matter of class relations was decisively influenced by personalities: Stalin, by his policies, was to bring about within a decade the split between peasantry and Party (if not working class) that Lenin had feared.

> man in the present Central Committee—but also by his too far-reaching self-confidence and by excessive enthusiasm for the purely administrative side of affairs. [In a subsequent passage Lenin refers parenthetically to Trotsky's "non-Bolshevism."]
>
> These two qualities of two prominent leaders of the present Central Committee [8] might inadvertently lead to a split; if our party does not take measures to prevent it, a split might arise unexpectedly.

The only measure Lenin proposed to prevent such a split, however, was enlargement of the Central Committee to fifty or a hundred members, which he had already recommended in the previous day's note.

In the balance of the December 24 note, Lenin characterized four other leaders. He recalled that Zinoviev and Kamenev, who were associated with Stalin in the incipient triumvirate, had opposed the decision to seize power in 1917 and this was "not accidental." He also characterized the strengths and weaknesses of Bukharin and Pyatakov, who were not members of the Politburo, while failing to mention Alexei Rykov and Michael Tomsky, who were.

As of December 25, the sense of Lenin's remarks was apparently as follows. The short-term danger of a split in the Party arises from the conflict between Stalin and Trotsky. Neither is suited for sole leadership, yet if they were to struggle for supremacy this could split the Party. Lenin seemed to warn the Party against accepting the rule of the incipient triumvirate of Zinoviev, Kamenev, and Stalin.

[8] Lenin's words are commonly rendered in English as "the two most able leaders of the C.C.," but he did not in fact use the superlative (*dvukh vidaiushchikhsia vozhdei*). On thc other hand, he did use the superlative in characterizing Bukharin and Pyatakov as "the most remarkable forces [*camie vidaiushchikhsia sili*] (among the youngest forces)," and in characterizing Trotsky as "the most able man in the present C.C." (*samii sposobnii chelovek v nastoiashchem Ts.K.*).

By noting Stalin's "enormous power" and attributing to him a political stature comparable to Trotsky's, while at the same time recalling Zinoviev's and Kamenev's great failure of will, Lenin indicated that the triumvirate was unstable. He may also have been warning Zinoviev and Kamenev that they were no match for their fellow triumvir.

The notes Lenin dictated in December for presentation to the Party's Congress offer in brief compass a penetrating analysis of the situation in the leadership. Although he called for "measures" to prevent a split, his sole explicit recommendation was to enlarge the Central Committee; doubtless this was not the only measure he thought necessary. When the letter was brought to their attention, the top leaders, and the Congress as a whole, were supposed to act on Lenin's analysis in the light of the then existing circumstances, which Lenin of course could not foresee.

Lenin did not leave it at that. His further reflections on the problem of succession were strongly affected by developments of the next eleven days. Midway in this interval, presumably on the basis of new information that had just reached him, Lenin dictated a memorandum on nationality policy in which he twice had occasion to criticize Stalin: "I think that a fatal role was played here by Stalin's hastiness and administrative impulsiveness, and also by his resentment against the notorious 'social-nationalism.' " On the related matter of repressive actions in the republic of Georgia, Lenin asked that Stalin (along with F. Dzerzhinsky, former Cheka head) be made "politically responsible for this truly Great Russian nationalist campaign." [9]

Shortly after completing this memorandum, on January

[9] *Kommunist,* No. 9 (June, 1956), pp. 22–25.

4, 1923, Lenin decided to add a new and decisive recommendation to his letter for the Congress on the matter of succession:

Stalin is too rude, and this fault, which is quite tolerable in our midst and in relations among us Communists, becomes intolerable in the office of General Secretary. Therefore, I propose to the comrades that they find a way to transfer Stalin from this post and appoint to it another man who in all other respects differs from Comrade Stalin in one advantage only, namely, that he be more tolerant, more loyal, more polite and more attentive to comrades, less capricious, etc. This circumstance could appear to be an insignificant trifle. I think, however, that from the viewpoint of preventing a split and from the viewpoint of what I have written above concerning the relationship between Stalin and Trotsky, this is not a trifle, or if it is one, then it is a trifle which can acquire a decisive significance.[10]

The qualities of Stalin mentioned in the postscript are not those criticized in the memorandum on nationality policy. The substance of the postscript may, therefore, also have been influenced by an incident involving Stalin and Krupskaya, Lenin's wife, which occurred on December 22. The incident was definitely known to Lenin by March 5, 1923, although he may or may not have known of it on January 4, when he dictated the postscript. Krupskaya reported the incident in a letter to Kamenev on December 23, 1922, in these words:

Lev Borisovich!
Because of a short letter which I had written in words dictated to me by Vladimir Ilyich by permission of the doctors, Stalin allowed himself yesterday an unusually rude outburst directed at me. This is not my first day in the Party. During all these thirty years I have never heard from any comrade one word of rudeness. The business of the Party and of Ilyich are not

[10] *Ibid.*, p. 18.

less dear to me than to Stalin. I need at present the maximum of self-control. What one can and what one cannot discuss with Ilyich—I know better than any doctor, because I know what makes him nervous and what does not, in any case I know better than Stalin. I am turning to you and to Grigory as to much closer comrades of V.I. and I beg you to protect me from rude interference with my private life and from vile invectives and threats. I have no doubt as to what will be the unanimous decision of the Control Commission, with which Stalin sees fit to threaten me; however, I have neither the strength nor the time to waste on this foolish quarrel. And I am a living person and my nerves are strained to the utmost.

Two and a half months later, in March, 1923, Lenin sent Stalin the following letter with copies to Kamenev and Zinoviev:

Dear Comrade Stalin!
You permitted yourself a rude summons of my wife to the telephone and a rude reprimand of her. Despite the fact that she told you that she agreed to forget what was said, nevertheless Zinoviev and Kamenev heard about it from her. I have no intention to forget so easily that which is being done against me, and I need not stress here that I consider as directed against me that which is being done against my wife. I ask you, therefore, that you weigh carefully whether you are agreeable to retracting your words and apologizing or whether you prefer the severance of relations between us.[11]

Whatever its cause, the effect of Lenin's postscript calling for Stalin's removal from the post of General Secretary was the abandonment of the neutrality between Stalin and Trotsky that Lenin had assumed in the previous notes. Stalin's capacity to arrogate power to himself and his tendency to employ it impulsively seemed to prey on Lenin's mind, and he now recommended that Stalin be deprived

[11] See Khrushchev's secret speech to the XX Congress in *The Anti-Stalin Campaign and International Communism* (New York, Columbia University Press, 1956), pp. 8–9.

of the position that was a key source of that power. Again, as in the rest of the letter, he assumed that his judgments about the leaders, and the recommendations that stemmed from them, would produce the required action at the proper time.

When Lenin began dictating his letter to the Party's Congress, he opened with this remark: "I should very much like to advise that a series of changes . . . be undertaken at this Congress";[12] he presumably meant the XII Congress, which was due to meet in March, 1923. Actually, the letter was to remain unknown to the principals until the following Congress, which met in May, 1924, several months after Lenin's death. A few days before the opening of this Congress, Krupskaya turned Lenin's letter over to Kamenev with a covering note in which she asserted that Lenin "expressed the definite wish that this note of his be submitted *after his death* to the next Party Congress."[13] It would appear that some time after December 23 (on which date he dictated only impersonal remarks on the need for organizational changes), Lenin decided that his letter should be withheld from the Party until after his death, and communicated his changed intention to Krupskaya. This could have occurred after Lenin had dictated his assessment of individual leaders on December 24 and 25, or after he had dictated his postscript calling for Stalin's removal as General Secretary on January 4. He could even have made this decision at some subsequent time, perhaps when he fell ill in the early days of March, or after his stroke, on March 9. His reasoning may have been

12 *Kommunist,* No. 9 (June, 1956), p. 16.

13 Emphasis added. Press release, June 30, 1956, in the U.S. Department of State *Bulletin,* Vol. XXXV, No. 891 (July 23, 1956), p. 153.

as follows: If he was incapacitated when the XII Congress met (in April, 1923, as it happened), and it failed to take the measures he proposed, particularly those affecting the power of individual leaders, his capacity to influence the succession might be decisively impaired; even if he were subsequently to recover, he might be reduced to being one of several contestants for power. On the other hand, if he recovered sufficiently to attend the XII Congress, or some subsequent one, he could himself present his proposals at that time. In short, having decided to name names, he also decided that if the letter was to be presented to the Party Congress by others acting on his behalf it should be only after his death.[14]

When the time came to present Lenin's letter to the Congress, seventeen months after he had written it, it passed from Krupskaya to Kamenev, who transmitted it to a Central Committee Plenum commission, made up of the triumvirate (Zinoviev, Kamenev, and Stalin) and three others who were not Politburo members. They in turn decided "to submit [the document] to the nearest Party Congress for its information." Nevertheless, the triumvirate managed first to bring the matter before "leaders of delegations to the Congress," who decided not only to retain Stalin in the post of General Secretary, but also to keep the letter from the Plenum of the Congress for whom Lenin had written it. Thus the Party leadership—though it honored Lenin's name by attaching it to the nation's second city, by quoting his writings and vowing to carry out his precepts, and by eulogizing his wisdom in a man-

[14] It cannot be excluded that Krupskaya lied when she said that Lenin wanted the letter transmitted after his death, but she seems to have had little reason to flaunt Lenin's true will and then misrepresent it.

ner that he had never permitted while alive—deliberately flouted the sole expression of Lenin's will that was made known to them after his death.

It is worth asking why Lenin, though he had ruled his followers in good measure by personal qualities—reasoned persuasion and a great reputation for political acumen—and had used coercion selectively and on the whole infrequently, could not effectuate his will after his death. Zinoviev and Kamenev, and their followers, doubtless knew that to reveal the letter to the Congress would destroy the triumvirate, and probably their own pretensions to rule as well. Stalin's ouster from the post of General Secretary would upset the new equilibrium of power that had been established after Lenin's incapacitation. In the ensuing struggle, Zinoviev and Kamenev would be at a disadvantage because of Lenin's judgment that their failure of will when the Bolsheviks seized power was characteristic of them.[15] Thus there was a divergence of will between Lenin, speaking through his testament, and the men who were supposed to be instruments of his will. This might have been foreseen by Lenin had he contrived his testament all of a piece, instead of in four separately dictated notes.

The part played by Trotsky, who had most to gain from publicizing the testament, was deeply ironical. In failing to employ the potent weapons Lenin had placed close to his hand, Trotsky fulfilled Lenin's judgment of him (one who "possesses an exaggerated self-confidence and excessive enthusiasm for the purely administrative side of affairs"), instead of fulfilling Lenin's will.

15 The most logical means of overcoming this disadvantage, an alliance with Trotsky, was anathema to them.

In the eighteen-month interval between the writing of Lenin's testament and its transmission to a small number of top leaders, the immediate consequences of Lenin's removal from the exercise of authority had largely worked themselves out and produced a new, though unstable, equilibrium. Throughout this period Trotsky, who had always benefited from Lenin's insistence on making full use of his talents, suffered a decline in both power and prestige. Stalin, while initially gaining from Lenin's removal from the scene in May, 1922, later was compromised by Lenin's criticism, especially in the memorandum on the nationality question which became known to a wide circle of readers. Had Lenin's testament been presented to the XII Congress (April, 1923), or had Lenin himself appeared there, Stalin might have suffered grave injury. Instead he succeeded in using his fellow triumvirs to cover his weakened position. They performed the same function for him again later in the year, when Trotsky launched an attack on the Party apparatus. Since they relied on the apparatus in their fight against Trotsky, Zinoviev and Kamenev defended it, and thereby its General Secretary. Subsequently, Stalin succeeded, because of his deep political sense and personal superiority to the vain and shallow Zinoviev, in gaining the pivotal position in the triumvirate.

POLICY DISPUTES

Lenin believed that the short-term danger to the regime arose from divisions within the leadership. The long-term danger, however, arose from divergent interests of the two main classes, the workers and the peasants, and could be averted only by means of a correct policy for the long term. It was necessary to bring the peasants to Socialism without provoking them to resistance. Were a split to occur in "the worker-peasant alliance," this could bring down the regime. Lenin directed himself to this problem in one of his last writings, "On Cooperatives."

In sum, Lenin pointed the direction, the socialization of agricultural production, but cautioned that the pace must be slow. His advice was good, but he failed to link the question of peasant policy with the question of personalities. While he had perceived Stalin's tendency to "hastiness and administrative impulsiveness" on a large question of policy (the national question), he apparently had no inkling that Stalin's display of these qualities, inflamed in the effort to consummate "a revolution from above," was to lead some years later to the disregard of his counsel, and consequently a turning of the peasantry against the regime. That this split of the "worker-peasant alliance" did not bring down the regime, as Lenin had feared it would, was perhaps due to Stalin's creation of instruments for preserving it that lay outside Lenin's political and moral world.[16]

All this lay a decade ahead, however. When Lenin wrote his cautionary essay in 1923, Stalin and his fellow triumvirs as yet remained determined to placate the peasant in accordance with the New Economic Policy (NEP) which had been initiated two years earlier. Just this question of whether to continue the NEP, however, was to become the great policy issue of the Lenin succession. Policy

[16] Lenin was by no means averse to the use of violence to seize and preserve power, but he seemed repelled by the idea of using violence as an instrument for creating Socialism.

toward the peasant was involved in the whole range of problems facing the regime, but especially the need for accumulating capital to industrialize the country. While the peasant question no doubt was inflamed by the struggle for Lenin's former power, it was no mere excuse for waging a power struggle. It concerned the fate of the Revolution.

When initiated in 1921, the NEP was conceived as an emergency measure to restore the economy. Its supporters included some who recognized the immediate necessity for it but looked forward to the time when it could be abandoned, and others who saw in NEP the basis for a gradual evolution toward Socialism. This issue remained latent until late 1923, when an acute crisis interrupted the economy's recovery. From that time until the succession was resolved, the top leadership was split on the question of whether to continue the pro-peasant NEP, or whether to shift to a policy of rapid socialization, both as a good in itself and as a means of achieving rapid industrialization.[17]

It has been argued in the West that divergences on this and other policy issues arose chiefly from power considerations. However, the interaction of power and policy is much less simple than this supposes. It is unlikely that Trotsky, who was the first to challenge NEP, in 1923, did so because he needed an issue on which to wage the power struggle. Until then, he had rigorously avoided a clash with the triumvirate, going so far as to throw aside the weapons that Lenin had placed in his hands for that purpose.

Power considerations doubtlessly played a great role in Zinoviev's decision, in 1925, to advocate a hardening of

[17] See A. Erlich, *The Soviet Industrialization Debate.*

the Party line on the peasantry; yet he may also have been influenced by the changed situation of the economy brought about by NEP. Industrial plants that had been made unproductive by the various upheavals from 1914 to 1921 had by 1925 been restored to production, so that new capital for plant expansion was becoming a pressing need. This raised the question of how, and at what rate, capital might be elicited from the privately operated agricultural economy. Zinoviev and Kamenev suffered an initial defeat in 1926 on their proposal to further industrialization at the expense of the peasantry (as well as on more narrowly power issues); together with their new ally, Trotsky, they met final defeat in 1927.

Now it became Stalin's turn to abandon NEP, a policy reversal which he accomplished in the course of the following year. Power considerations no doubt played a great part in Stalin's turn to the Left in 1928. First, not till then, probably, could he have succeeded in getting a Leftist line adopted without entering into compromises with the Left Opposition. Stalin's turn to the Left also made it easier for him to be rid of the Rightists, who remained on the Politburo. At the same time, it is also true that Stalin was faced with a new food crisis in 1928, which evidently required either new concessions to the peasantry or new measures to be applied against them. It would be hard to show that Stalin's motive was simply to consolidate his power, and that he was not convinced that new concessions to the peasantry would endanger the Party's hold on the economy.

Whatever the anatomy of the victor's motivation, in the struggle of the defeated, policy considerations had considerable weight. Trotsky's position was basically consistent throughout the period of the 1920s, so that even at the end he found his great antagonist, Stalin, preferable to the Rightists.[18] The Rightists, too, were largely consistent throughout. They observed Stalin's build-up of a powerful machine that crushed his opponents one after another without making any serious effort to build up countervailing power. Only when Stalin had turned this machine into a legislative mechanism whose laws they disapproved of, did they turn against Stalin. Even then, they did not change their policy in order to facilitate an alliance with those whom Stalin had already defeated, as pure power politics would have directed. Instead, they found themselves defending, in isolation, the program they believed best for the Party and the country.

In retrospect, the Lenin succession appears as a period in which the most fundamental problems could not be resolved, owing to the lack of a clear center of decision and to the related need of maintaining a concessionary policy toward the people. While Stalin's power had grown steadily after 1923, not until 1928 was he in a position to initiate radically new policies; even then, two more years were required for him to consolidate his dictatorial power.

The struggle over economic policy during the Lenin succession yields certain provisional generalizations. The effects of fundamental issues on succession are rather more complicated than might be supposed. Initially, such issues do tend to exacerbate factional conflict. Individuals and factions are compelled to take a position, and this tends to polarize the leadership. Moreover, personal interest as a motive for struggle may be strongly reinforced by regard

[18] Trotsky did become critical in the early 1930s of Stalin's ruinous pace in collectivizing and in forcing the development of industry, but this was no departure from his earlier program.

for Party interests. In the later stages of succession, however, such issues may attenuate conflict by preventing defeated factions from combining to renew the struggle on the basis of a common policy; or, if the attempt at combination succeeds, the alliance may be vulnerable and quickly defeated because of its lack of common principles.

One further point. While issues can be manufactured during a succession struggle, there are usually enough genuine ones available to make this unnecessary.

THE RULING BODIES

We have seen that, while Lenin still ruled, he exercised his power through both the Party and the government. In the Party, formally, he had no special position but was simply a member of the Politburo along with six others; he headed the government, however, as Chairman of the Council of People's Commissars. He governed through the state apparatus directly, through the Party apparatus indirectly. The government's prestige stemmed chiefly from Lenin's position as its head, so that its authority inevitably declined as he withdrew from affairs. The Party, as the embodiment of Revolutionary will, decided overall policy. The locus of decision-making was the Politburo (and in some degree the Central Committee), not the Party apparatus, or its center, the Secretariat.

In his last writings, Lenin did not limit himself to the attempt to influence the distribution of power among his heirs. He also sought to influence the distribution of power among the various ruling bodies. His proposal for an expanded Central Committee, which was made in several of his writings at this time and became widely known, was at least in part an appeal not to distribute his former powers among a very few leaders, but rather to disperse them in an enlarged and strengthened Central Committee.

Of necessity, some dispersal of power did occur. Lenin's personal dictatorship was succeeded for a few years by an oligarchy or "collective leadership." At first, it was made up of three bodies, the two smaller within the largest. The largest, but *least* powerful, was the Central Committee. A sign of its oligarchical status was the stable tenure of its members: almost all who were elected to it in 1922 were still on it in 1926. That its status as an oligarchical body was quite low, however, appears from the fact that during this period the Central Committee's membership almost doubled (from twenty-seven to fifty-three). Superficially, this was in accord with Lenin's intention. But though it increased the Central Committee's members, the Party Congress failed to provide the Central Committee with Lenin's former powers. In fact, since the new members were not co-opted but were nominated by a smaller body, who thereby influenced its composition, the Central Committee increasingly lost what independence it had.

The next oligarchical body was the Politburo of the Central Committee. From 1922 until 1926, it had a fixed number of members (seven). No one was removed from the Politburo during this period, and the only new member, Bukharin, was added to replace Lenin after his death. The Politburo remained the effective policy-making agency during this period, partly through its control over the Central Committee. Nevertheless, the Politburo was not the supreme oligarchical body. Lenin's enforced absence from its deliberations deprived the Politburo of much of its former authority, and in time it came to be dominated by the triumvirate, whom Stalin spoke of as "the core that has been formed within the Central Committee in the course of years of work."[19] Moreover, the tenure of Politburo members in the first period of succession had a fragile basis: it was as though they kept their places because Lenin had placed them there. Membership on the Politburo was no guarantee against loss of influence. The effective power of Trotsky was so far reduced by mid-1924 that he was not even allowed to vote at the XIII Congress.

Gradually, as Stalin's ascendancy grew, it became clear that the really decisive body was not the Politburo or the triumvirate within it, but the Secretariat of the Central Committee, which Stalin had made fundamentally an extension of his own will. By 1926 the Secretariat had gained control over the entire Party apparatus; by 1928 it had become the means whereby Stalin could determine national policy; by 1930 it had removed Stalin's opponents from the Politburo, which now approved his proposals unanimously.

BASES OF POWER

Political struggle, such as occurs during succession, is waged by the contending leaders and factions by means of various political agencies, bases of power, that are at their disposal: national institutions, territorial organizations and constituencies, social groups, and so forth. What were the power bases of the contestants in the Lenin succession?

When Trotsky moved to challenge the triumvirate's

[19] J. V. Stalin, *Works* (Moscow, Foreign Languages Publishing House, 1953), V, 231.

policies late in 1923, several impressive power bases were available to him. He had great prestige among the regime's supporters as the executor of Lenin's strategy in making the October Revolution and as the creator of the Red Army. His popularity was especially great among students in the Komsomol. Trotsky was War Commissar and had many supporters in its upper ranks. Many of the Party's top planners and economic administrators were his personal supporters, besides being sharply critical of the triumvirate's economic policies. Until mid-1923, at any rate, Trotsky was also in a position to control the Ukraine, which was headed by one of his closest adherents, Christian Rakovsky.

Despite his influence among these groups, Trotsky proved unable to make good use of them. He did not use his position in the army to advantage, out of fear of stimulating the already widespread suspicion that he had Bonapartist tendencies, and by 1925 he had been ousted from the War Commissariat. Trotsky made his boldest appeal for support to young intellectuals in the Komsomol, but it was effectively countered by the triumvirate through its control of the central Party apparatus and the major provincial organizations. In intra-Party maneuvering, Trotsky proved to be a poor strategist as well as a poor tactician. In part, this weakness stemmed from his extreme self-confidence, which Lenin had noted; yet it may also have been due to his belief in the decisive character of ebbs and flows in the revolutionary spirit of the masses, a belief which left little place for factional politics and appeals to interest groups. Whatever the reason for his ineptness, he dissipated his strength in attacks on the wrong opponents: in 1924 he attacked Zinoviev and Kamenev, instead of Stalin;

in 1928 he attacked Stalin's Rightist opponents, instead of the archenemy himself.

Trotsky's incapacity for political in-fighting had already been demonstrated by early 1924, when he suffered a Party reprimand. By the end of the year his position had been seriously compromised. For the time being, he retired from the fray.

The triumvirate was an informal body, not a real collective. Its rule was based on the aggregate power of its several members. This meant, however, that its preservation very much depended upon the balance of power among the individuals who made it up. Stalin controlled the central Party apparatus in Moscow, the Secretariat and its powerful staff, which gained greatly in independence from Lenin's illness. As already noted, the concentration of power during the last half of 1922 in the Secretariat, and more particularly in its General Secretary, Stalin, had disturbed Lenin. His efforts to undo this development, however, had at best slowed its progress. The other two triumvirs, Zinoviev and Kamenev (who throughout remained close allies), were the respective satraps of Leningrad and Moscow, and controlled the various mechanisms of provincial power in those cities. They dominated the local Party machines, not directly in their own persons, but through deputies: P. Zalutsky, the Secretary in Leningrad, and I. Zelensky, the Secretary in Moscow. In 1925 Stalin moved to destroy his fellow triumvirs. He captured provincial power in Moscow from Kamenev; shortly afterwards, at the beginning of 1926, he took the Leningrad organization from Zinoviev. In both instances the Party apparatus was then subordinated to the Central Committee's Secretariat, that is to say, made subject to Stalin's will. The concentration of power in the central Party apparatus was thus coincident with the concentration of power in Stalin's person, and was in fact the chief means whereby Stalin gained the commanding heights of the Party.

By 1926 Stalin had destroyed the triumvirate, but he had not yet established his unchallenged supremacy. Zinoviev and Kamenev soon allied themselves with Trotsky and returned to battle against the Rightists, led by Stalin. Now, however, they had to do battle without effective political weapons. Their efforts to appeal to the rank-and-file membership against its leader were at once pathetic and, at least on Trotsky's part, impressive, even noble. In any case they were foredoomed if for no other reason than that half of those in the Party in 1926 were new to it. The new members had been recruited after Lenin's death largely by Stalin's Party machine, and they knew where their allegiance belonged. The situation is well described by Victor Serge, a one-time Trotskyist:

> I was a member of the party cell at the *Krasnaya Gazeta,* the big evening newspaper [in Leningrad]. . . . There were about 400 of us. . . . Three Old Bolsheviks, lost in this multitude, occupied managerial posts. Ten or so comrades had been in the Civil War. The other 387 (or thereabouts) were from the "Lenin enrolment": workers who had joined the Party only at the death of Lenin, after the consolidation of power and at the height of NEP. We Oppositionists numbered five, one of whom was shaky; we were all of the Civil War generation. It was a miniature of the situation in the Party as a whole; many things are explained thereby.[20]

After a series of defeats without victories, the united Op-

[20] Victor Serge, *Memoirs of a Revolutionary,* tr. by Peter Sedgwick (London, Oxford University Press, 1963), pp. 214–15.

position was finally crushed at the XV Party Congress, in late 1927. Zinoviev and Kamenev abjectly surrendered in order to remain in the Party, while Trotsky, politically isolated once more, passed into tragic exile.

From the onset of the NEP (1921), the Party's basic policy had been Rightist. Trotsky was the first to diverge from it; then Zinoviev and Kamenev; finally, Stalin himself. When Stalin split away from the NEP policy in 1928, however, he carried with him the Party. Still, the remaining supporters of NEP included some well-known figures: Rykov, head of the government; Tomsky, head of the trade unions; and Bukharin, official ideologist and theoretician of the Right Wing. In addition, the effective head of the political police, G. Yagoda, was a secret sympathizer with the Right, and the head of the Moscow Party organization, N. Uglanov, openly supported it. But Uglanov was quickly removed from his position, and Yagoda's sympathies seemingly proved of little value to the Right Opposition.

Of the institutions that the Right Opposition could try to use, the government was probably the most important, although it too had serious weaknesses. The government bureaucracy comprised numerous tsarist holdovers, and had been castigated repeatedly by Lenin for its ignorance, inertia, and lukewarm allegiance to the Soviet regime. While the Party had a sacred and prestigious aura, even apart from Lenin's leadership of it, the government did not. As already noted, its authority began to decline as soon as Lenin fell ill. As early as the autumn of 1922, Trotsky declined a proposal of Lenin's that he become deputy chairman of the Council of People's Commissars on the ground that Party functionaries were making decisions behind the backs of the responsible commissars.[21]

Throughout the 1920s, Stalin found the government a far less reliable instrument than the Party apparatus. According to a leading student of the period:

> Of the prominent Party members listed in the index of names and the protocols of the Eleventh Party Congress, only sixteen percent of those in Party work became oppositionists, by 1930, whereas fifty percent of those working in the government and other institutions found themselves in one deviation or another by that time.[22]

Not much is known of the use actually made of the government by the Right Opposition. According to Stalin, however, Rykov on a number of occasions used the authority of the government for illicit Rightist purposes.[23] While Stalin's charge may be groundless, it seems likely that to the extent the Right carried its fight outside the meetings of the Politburo and the Central Committee, it did use the bases of power that were available to it, including the government.

[21] In reporting this incident several years later, Trotsky interpreted Lenin's proposal to mean his designation as heir apparent. Lenin proposed the formation of a commission which was to become "the lever for breaking up the Stalin faction as the backbone of the bureaucracy, and for creating such conditions in the party as would allow me to become Lenin's deputy and, as he intended, his successor to the post of Chairman of the People's Commissaries [*sic*]. Only in this connection does the full meaning of the so-called 'Will' become clear. Unquestionably, his object in making the will was to facilitate the work of direction for me. . . . It rounds out and clarifies the proposal that Lenin made me in our last conversation." Leon Trotsky, *My Life* (New York, Scribners, 1930), pp. 479–80. Believing this, Trotsky nevertheless declined the post offered him and later failed to use the testament as Lenin had intended. Here was a would-be king who insisted that others must place the crown on his head; Stalin was not so particular.

[22] R. Daniels, *Conscience of the Revolution* (Cambridge, Harvard University Press, 1960), p. 170.

[23] J. V. Stalin, *Works,* XII, 107–9.

Since its own resources were inadequate for the fight against Stalin, it was crucial that the Right find allies. Two strategies were open to its leaders in opposing Stalin's move to the Left. First, they could seek an alliance with the former Left Opposition that was directed against Stalin personally, rather than against his policy. This they actually attempted, in July, 1928. Bukharin, having finally come to know Stalin as an opponent, secretly visited Kamenev and said: "What can one do before an adversary of this type: a Ghengis Khan?" His approach was rebuffed, however, and subsequently was exposed by the Trotskyists, who preferred Stalin to the Rightists.[24]

A second strategy was open to the Right Opposition. In opposing forced collectivization and breakneck industrialization, it could seek allies among the less doctrinaire members of the Party, as well as among broad social groups opposed to Stalin's program. According to Victor Serge: "The Right Opposition was more of a state of mind than an organization; at certain junctures it included the great majority of officials and enjoyed the sympathy of the whole nation." If the Right's leaders in the Politburo had placed themselves at the head of these multitudinous officials and of the nation, they might have succeeded in blocking Stalin's program, and perhaps in unseating him as well. Yet they made no attempt to do so. The reason is simple. The Party of the proletariat was weak in a predominantly peasant nation, and the Right feared that by turning to the

[24] "One of the last actions of our Moscow 'Centre' had been the publication, in 1928, of pamphlets which told of the confidential discussions between Bukharin and Kamenev. . . . Our [Trotskyist] 'Centre' (B. M. Eltsin) may very well have much to answer for in publishing these documents. From that moment onward, the Right of Bukharin, Rykov, and Tomsky is *de facto* ousted from power." Victor Serge, *Memoirs of a Revolutionary*, pp. 258–59.

people for support they would set forces in motion that might bring about the Party's overthrow.

Afraid of the sources of their own strength, and rebuffed by Stalin's Leftist foes, the Right Opposition suffered almost total defeat within a relatively short time. Stalin discredited its leaders before the Central Committee, which he controlled, and then at his leisure proceeded to deprive them of the positions that conferred whatever political strength remained to them.

In the new Politburo elected in 1930 only one member remained from Lenin's day. Stalin had made himself supreme ruler, and thus resolved the Lenin succession crisis. The legitimacy of his rule was established in the only way possible in a newly founded regime: Stalin ruled as Lenin's closest comrade in arms, as the continuer of Lenin's great cause. As a later slogan had it: Stalin is Lenin today.

THE OUTCOME

Lenin's effort to influence the succession with respect to personalities, policy, and organization met complete defeat. His advice, offered after serious deliberation and with due gravity, was disregarded even while he lived by men who professed to revere him. They not only failed to act on Lenin's recommendations; they also failed to learn from the arguments by which he justified them. Stalin, however, may be an exception to this; Lenin's testament may have taught him caution and dissimulation even beyond what was natural to him.

Lenin's last writings had not exhausted their historical significance in 1930. A third of a century late, they were finally handed over to the Party's Congress by a new pretender to Lenin's mantle, who had learned that his ambitions could be advanced by attacking Stalin.

Khrushchev's use of Lenin's testament in 1956 serves as a reminder that it remained an important part of the Soviet political scene even after the XIII Congress decided to suppress it. It was widely known in Party circles and for a time was often alluded to at Party meetings by the principals. As late as 1932, when Stalin had brought the country almost to the verge of disaster, an opposition group headed by M. Riutin called for Stalin's removal as General Secretary of the Central Committee. Stalin evidently felt so threatened by this echo of Lenin's testament that he demanded that Riutin be executed. This was at first denied him because of the unwritten Party law that the blood of Bolsheviks must not be spilled by the Party,[25] and Riutin was merely imprisoned. Four years later, almost to the day, Stalin demanded a widespread purge, complaining that it was four years overdue.[26]

Was the great purge of the 1930s, then, a final event in the Lenin succession? In a sense, perhaps, it was. Lenin had failed to effectuate his testament, but it remained a threat to Stalin's rule for it gave the lie to his chief claim to legitimacy. If the country were once more to sink as low as in 1932, perhaps as a result of defeat in war, Stalin's opponents doubtless would use the testament against him if they could, and Stalin's deification of Lenin would only

[25] A few years previously an Oppositionist, Yakov Bliumkin, had been executed, but this was apparently because he had failed to carry out an assignment of the political police. Serge, *Memoirs of a Revolutionary*, p. 257.

[26] See the commentary on the secret speech by Boris Nicolaevsky in *The New Leader* (July 16, 1956), p. S23 (in Special Section Two).

give the testament greater authority. The testament may be taken as the symbol, if nothing more, of all the good reasons Stalin had for destroying numerous Old Bolsheviks, and even for wiping out the Party apparatus which had raised him to supremacy in open disregard of Lenin's will.[27]

After the purge was over, in 1938, Stalin made a new effort to efface the stigma that Lenin had placed on his rule. There could of course be no point in publicly denying that Lenin had called for his removal as General Secretary, since by then the very existence of the testament was known to relatively few. Instead, Stalin invented the myth that it was Lenin who had proposed him as General Secretary in the first place. This myth was incorporated in the new official history of the Party in 1938, and was repeated on suitable occasions even after Stalin died. Since 1956, however, the myth has disappeared from Soviet pages, as though bringing to light Lenin's testament had dispelled it.

[27] One wonders whether Stalin's unwillingness to make himself head of the government until 1941 may owe something to the testament's power over his mind.

III: The Stalin Succession

The Stalin succession, looked at retrospectively, has marked similarities to the Lenin succession.[1] Yet the principals, on the evidence of their actions, were not aware that they were largely reenacting the Lenin succession. They apparently supposed that conditions had been so altered during the three decades of Stalin's rule that the keys to power were no longer what they had been. There was but a single exception. Nikita Khrushchev deliberately patterned his strategy on the one Stalin had followed after Lenin's mortal illness. Like Stalin, Khrushchev achieved his goal.

In early March, 1953, Moscow announced that Stalin had suffered a stroke, and two days later that he was dead. Foreign observers who had seen him two weeks earlier testify to his good health at that time, so his death and the problem of succession came suddenly upon the Soviet

1 While a comprehensive history of the Stalin succession remains to be written, several useful accounts have appeared, among them: R. Conquest, *Power and Policy in the USSR* (New York, St. Martin's Press, 1961); W. Leonhard, *The Kremlin Since Stalin* (New York, Praeger, 1962); R. Tucker, *The Soviet Political Mind* (New York, Praeger, 1963); B. Wolfe, *Khrushchev and Stalin's Ghost* (New York, Praeger, 1957). There is a good brief account in Robert H. McNeal, *The Bolshevik Tradition* (Englewood, N.J., Prentice-Hall, 1963), 144–60. I have discussed some of the points raised in this chapter at greater length in *The Rise of Khrushchev* (Washington, D.C., Public Affairs Press, 1958).

scene. In this it differs from the Lenin succession, which began as a period of uncertainty about Lenin's capacity to rule and deepened with the passage of time. In both cases the death of the supreme ruler had been preceded by preliminary maneuvering for the succession. While Lenin participated as a prestigious invalid, however, Stalin, though aged, did so while still able-bodied and in possession of his faculties, and was thus able to dominate the early maneuvering for succession. On the whole, Stalin had somewhat greater success than Lenin in projecting his will into the period of succession, yet on the question that was decisive for him—the perpetuation of his personal glory—he suffered total defeat.

Stalin was sixty-five when World War II ended, and seventy-three at the time of his death. During this interval, and particularly towards its end, he showed concern about the succession, although he may well have hoped to live many more years. In any case, his chief preoccupation was assuredly the continued exercise of his own authority rather than arranging its transfer to his heirs, so that the need to preserve his own vast power intact narrowly limited his succession arrangements. These arrangements were broadly of three kinds, pertaining to institutions, policy, and personnel.

Stalin's heritage was largely embodied in the institutions he had created. When the Lenin succession began in 1922 Soviet institutions were still in their formative stage; after three decades of Stalin's rule they had largely been established. Lenin's efforts to arrange the succession were designed to preserve the conditions that would make possible the realization of Socialism; Stalin's were designed to preserve what he had wrought. This is reflected in the conservatism of Stalin's last work, "Economic Problems of Socialism in the USSR,"[2] which still acknowledges the need for a further transformation of Soviet society, but with the watchwords "caution" and "gradualness." Stalin now rejects the earlier orthodoxy which affirmed the power of the Soviet state to transform society. Instead, he stresses the limits imposed on action by the law-bound regularities of social existence, as though he feels it necessary to warn his heirs against tampering with the system he had created. His forebodings were to be justified by subsequent events.

Stalin's final prescriptions for long-term policy are also to be found in the "Economic Problems of Socialism." He felt able to prescribe freely since this did not require him to give up anything of his present power, and even served to enhance his authority and to limit the views which others might express. In part the work is polemical, being directed against views which had some currency at that time, but their object was not merely to set straight the current line. In keeping with his latter-day conservatism, he sought to make such views anathema so as to lessen the likelihood of their being adopted by his successors. Since Stalin made no further extended pronouncements, his views as expressed in the "Economic Problems" may be taken as a final, if rather limited, testament for his heirs. It is therefore worthwhile stating them, and briefly indicating what their fate was to be after his death.

The "Economic Problems" provided an analysis of the state of the world and a doctrinal statement on the preconditions for transition to Communism, both of which im-

[2] First published in *Bolshevik,* No. 18 (1952); later issued as a separate work.

plied prescriptions for long-term policy. His analysis of the state of the world was optimistic and served to justify the foreign policy he had established. According to Stalin, the relative stability which capitalism had achieved after World War I no longer existed. Imperialism would inevitably give rise to wars which were likely to involve the capitalist countries, not the USSR.

The analysis seemed to imply that the USSR need not attempt to stimulate divisions between capitalist states, but could rely on divisive forces that were inherent within the capitalist world to weaken it.[3] Apparently Stalin continued to look to war and the threat of war, rather than to revolution, as the chief means of spreading Communism. Moreover, his confidence that the USSR was not in danger of attack seemed to make it unnecessary to seek a significant lessening of international tensions, and perhaps encouraged the belief that aggressive actions could be undertaken against the West without incurring great risks. The grounds of this confidence may have been Stalin's awareness of the destructiveness of modern weapons. It is often forgotten that Stalin's recognition, at the end of World War II, of the military potentialities of modern technology led to the initiation of top-priority development programs that were to provide his successors, within a few months of his death, with thermonuclear weapons, intercontinental bombers, and short-range ballistic missiles. Had Stalin lived, it is possible that these new weapons would have been made the basis for a new and more aggressive political offensive against the West.

Stalin's assessment of the world situation probably did

[3] See translation in *Current Soviet Policies*, ed. by L. Gruliow (New York, Praeger, 1953), pp. 7–8.

influence his heirs, or at least a faction among them, for a brief period after his death. By the beginning of 1955, however, there were increasing signs of their departure from his precepts. This is reflected, for example, in the fact that Molotov, Stalin's most faithful heir, became increasingly isolated within the leadership on questions of foreign policy. Stalin's dictum on the instability of the capitalist world, while not explicitly abandoned, ceased to be a supposition of Soviet foreign policy, while his dictum on the likelihood of wars among capitalist states seems inconsistent with the doctrine enunciated in 1956 that wars are no longer fatalistically inevitable.

Elsewhere in the "Economic Problems of Socialism" Stalin stated the conditions for the transition to Communism and outlined the policies necessary to achieve them.[4] First, it was necessary that the production of capital goods increase more rapidly than the production of consumer goods. Second, collective farming had to be gradually eliminated by being "elevated" to the level of public (state) property. This was to be achieved by gradually restricting collective farm production for the market (for money) and fostering production of goods for exchange with other enterprises (product exchange). The new system was to be "introduced without particular haste" but "steadily, unwaveringly, without hesitation, step by step." Third, education must advance to a point where members of society could exercise a free choice of occupation and not be confined to a single occupation. For this leisure was needed (a five-hour work day), radically improved housing, and a doubled standard of living.

[4] *Ibid.*, p. 14.

Stalin's purpose in stating these conditions was polemical and conservative. He wanted to demonstrate the difficulty of the task and to establish how to go about it.[5] Within a few months after Stalin's death, however, Stalin's "Economic Problems of Socialism" had virtually dropped from sight. The XX Party Congress (February, 1956) did not enact Stalin's program; its attention was drawn to Stalin's article only by Mikoyan, who spoke of its shortcomings. A few days after Mikoyan's remarks, whatever chance remained that Stalin might yet pass into history as the Legislator of Soviet Communism was dispelled by Khrushchev in his secret speech of February 25, 1956.

From then on, not only were Stalin's prescriptions ignored but his injunctions were flouted, as when Khrushchev, in 1958, abolished the Machine Tractor Stations (M.T.S.) and enabled the collective farms to buy their equipment. In "Economic Problems" Stalin had argued against this step, not only for the sake of expediency, but, more important, on the grounds that it was "incompatible with the prospect of transition from Socialism to Communism." To think otherwise, he said, "is a profound blunder [arising] from lack of understanding of Marxism." Undeterred by Stalin's prohibition, indeed without referring to it, Khrushchev proclaimed that in abolishing the M.T.S. the Soviet Union was advancing toward Communism. Subsequently the Party disregarded Stalin's warnings about the great difficulty and complexity of achieving Communism by adopting a program which called for

[5] Even the Congress' resolution establishing a commission to revise the Party program, while it instructed the Commission to be guided by the fundamental theses of the "Economic Problems," said nothing of achieving Communism.

building its foundations within two decades, at the same time rejecting measures that Stalin had insisted were necessary.

One major precept of Stalin's last writing, however, was heeded: this was the injunction to give continuing priority to production of capital goods. As late as 1955 Stalin's words were invoked against Malenkov and his partisans, who sought to violate it.[6] Even at this writing, the precept, in word and deed, still stands.

In his personnel arrangements for the succession Stalin was more cautious, since they had a close bearing on his current power. After World War II, it appeared for a time that Andrei Zhdanov might be the heir presumptive, since his power rose while that of his chief rival, Malenkov, declined. The opposite occurred in the first half of 1948, however: Zhdanov's position was weakened, and Malenkov returned to the Secretariat after an absence of two years. Stalin thus made Malenkov the only figure besides himself to sit in the three top councils—Secretariat, Council of Ministers, and Politburo—which seemed to mark him more clearly than anyone had been previously as Stalin's intended successor. Zhdanov's death in August, 1948, however, and the subsequent purge of Zhdanovites from the Leningrad Party organization, threatened to unbalance the arrangement of power among Stalin's lieutenants by giving Malenkov too much. In December, 1949, Stalin brought Khrushchev from the Ukraine to Moscow. He became the third member of the Politburo in the central Secretariat, the others being Stalin and Malenkov, and was also chosen to head the Moscow provincial Party or-

[6] See the article in *Pravda* by its then editor, D. Shepilov, on January 24, 1955.

ganization. In this way Stalin created a powerful counterweight to Malenkov's extraordinary powers. A triad had been formed with Stalin as dictator, Malenkov as heir presumptive, and Khrushchev.[7] The triadic succession arrangement was confirmed in 1952 at the XIX Party Congress, when Malenkov gave the Report of the Central Committee and Khrushchev gave the next most important report, one on changes in the Party statute.

Khrushchev's role in the triad was to block any effort by Malenkov to seize greater power than Stalin meant him to have.[8] He was a counter heir, not, apparently, an alternate heir. Stalin seemed to lack confidence in Khrushchev's capacity to realize a grand policy, for the responsibilities given him had been chiefly administrative and had involved policy only in limited areas, such as agriculture. Significantly, when a commission was set up by the XIX Party Congress to draft a new Party program, Khrushchev was not included among its eleven members. Nevertheless, when Stalin died a few months later, Khrushchev succeeded in using the power Stalin had conferred upon him to establish himself as a rival claimant for the succession.

In his arrangements for the succession, Stalin, a morbidly suspicious despot, did not simply transfer power from his own hands. Paralleling the measures concentrating power in the two subordinate members of the triad

[7] Of course, important residual power existed outside this triadic succession arrangement (though largely in fragmented form) in the intricate system of checks and balances by which Stalin ruled in his last years. A triad of this type, in which the first member is a dictator, must be distinguished from a troika, or triumvirate, whose members are relatively equal in power.

[8] As noted later (pp. 53 and 54), Khrushchev's protégés were given key posts in the political police, especially after 1951.

were measures that increased Stalin's direct control over affairs. These measures were of two kinds, a rearrangement of the top Party bodies and moves to reinstitute the public blood purge.

Stalin's special position in the leadership was accentuated by a reorganization of the Party's executive bodies at the time of the XIX Party Congress (October, 1952), which at the same time reduced the status of his senior subordinates. An enlarged Presidium of twenty-five members was elected, replacing the former Politburo, which had numbered ten; the Secretariat was also increased, from four to ten. Stalin continued to be first in the listing of the members of these bodies, but now the other names were listed *alphabetically,* instead of in rank order as before.[9] This eliminated distinctions among the senior lieutenants, reducing them all to a level along with the new members, and emphasized Stalin's special position above all the others.

Paralleling these measures to reassert his supremacy were others by which Stalin prepared a blood purge of top subordinates. In late 1951, the head of the Ministry of State Security, V. Abakumov, a long-time political official, was replaced by S. Ignatiev, who was new to this profession and worked directly under Stalin's orders. Approximately a year later, in mid-January, 1953, "the doctor-affair" broke upon the Soviet political scene.[10] A number of doctors, most of them Jewish, were arrested as agents of foreign intelligence agencies who had allegedly sabotaged the treatment of public figures in the USSR in order to shorten their lives. Shortly after Stalin's death

9 *Pravda,* October 17, 1952.
10 *Pravda,* January 13, 1953.

it was officially announced that this whole affair was a fabrication.[11] It seems clear that the doctor-affair was authored by Stalin, and was directed against top level leaders of the USSR. While the maneuver involved a reassertion of Stalin's autocratic rule, it also had a crucial bearing on the triadic succession arrangements outlined above. Yet even now, more than a decade later, it is not clear how the doctor-affair was meant to affect the disposition of power within the triad and, more broadly, among Stalin's lieutenants.

Khrushchev raised just this question of Stalin's intentions toward his senior lieutenants and future successors in his last months. Because Khrushchev's role in these events may be an important issue in the Khrushchev succession, we must consider his expressed views at some length. According to Khrushchev, in the secret speech against Stalin at the XX Congress:

> His proposal, after the XIXth Congress concerning the selection of 25 persons to the Central Committee Presidium, was aimed at the removal of the old Political Bureau members. . . . We can assume that this was also a design for the future annihilation of the old Political Bureau members and in this way a cover for all shameful acts of Stalin, acts which we are now considering.[12]

If this was Stalin's intention, he was embarking upon a course that was not only dangerous, but foolishly so. Even the great blood purge of the 1930s wiped out no more than half Stalin's Politburo. It is hard to believe that this master of bloody intrigue would have moved against the entire Politburo at once, rather than creating divisions

11 *Pravda,* April 4, 1953.

12 *The Anti-Stalin Campaign and International Communism* (New York, Columbia University Press, 1956), p. 85.

among them and securing allies for himself. One wonders whether Khrushchev was not adding to the number of Stalin's intended victims for reasons of his own.

When Khrushchev in the secret speech came to the doctor-affair, on the other hand, he said nothing of its being directed against Stalin's closest subordinates. Stalin was accused of setting up the case, but he was made to appear as a victim of his own suspicious nature. Stalin had received a letter from a woman doctor in which:

> She declared that doctors were applying supposedly improper methods of medical treatment. Such a letter was sufficient for Stalin to reach an immediate conclusion that there were doctor-plotters in the Soviet Union. He issued orders to arrest a group of eminent Soviet medical specialists.[13]

While the woman doctor who sent the letter "was probably influenced or ordered by someone" to write it, Khrushchev gave no hint as to who this "someone" might have been. Stalin was not responsible for the letter, in his account, but was moved to action by it; neither was Beria, whom Khrushchev accused of almost every possible crime. (Subsequently Beria was inculpated, which suggests that Khrushchev's account was patently unsatisfactory.) [14] Who then "influenced or ordered" the woman doctor to write it? In Khrushchev's version Stalin did not intend to make the doctor-affair the basis for charges that his subordinates were plotting against him; he treated them as innocents, not as criminals.

> Shortly after the doctors were arrested we members of the Political Bureau [15] received protocols with the doctors' con-

[13] *Ibid.*, pp. 63–64.

[14] *Pravda,* July 8, 1956.

[15] This suggests that the old Political Bureau continued to meet separately after the Presidium was set up.

fessions of guilt. After distributing these protocols Stalin told us, "You are blind like young kittens; what will happen without me? The country will perish because you do not know how to recognize enemies." [16]

There is, then, this difficulty in Khrushchev's account of Stalin's last months: he asserted that Stalin meant to annihilate the old Politburo, yet he linked this design with the enlargement of the Party's executive body, not with the doctor-affair. One cannot but wonder why Khrushchev treated the doctor-affair as pertaining only to the accused doctors, and said nothing of its implications for Stalin's lieutenants and future successors.[17]

There are also bits of positive evidence pointing towards Khrushchev's involvement in the fabricated doctor-affair. The question is of more than historical interest, since Khrushchev may yet be charged with complicity in the doctor-affair now that he has passed from the political scene. Perhaps the most striking evidence bearing on Khrushchev's involvement in the doctor-affair is the strong representation in the political police at that time of men he had patronized.

The Minister of State Security at that time, S. Ignatiev, who was politically discredited for his role in the doctor-affair when Beria was ascendant, was appointed First Secretary in the Bashkir Republic when Khrushchev took charge of the Party apparatus. Subsequently Khrushchev defended Ignatiev and his key deputy, M. Riumin, who had been responsible for "special investigations." Accord-

[16] *Anti-Stalin Campaign,* p. 64.

[17] Moreover, Khrushchev said nothing of the specific charges against the doctors: that they had murdered A. Shcherbakov and A. Zhdanov and had conspired to murder a number of top Soviet military leaders who were identified by name.

ing to the secret speech, Ignatiev had been told by Stalin: "If you do not obtain confessions from the doctors, we shall shorten you by a head." Riumin had been instructed on how to get those confessions: "These methods were simple—beat, and beat, and beat again."

Ignatiev's other deputies in January, 1953, included I. Serov, who had served under Khrushchev as head of the Ukrainian political police, and who later protected Khrushchev's person and served his factional interests as head of the Soviet political police during the Stalin succession; A. Yepishev, who was brought from Kiev in 1951 to serve as Ignatiev's deputy, and who, in 1962, was appointed Party watchdog over the armed forces; and N. Mironov, who was brought from the Ukraine in 1951 to serve in the political police, and who became Party watchdog over the political police.

The coincidence that five of Khrushchev's protégés were in the political police at the time of the doctor-affair and that Khrushchev went out of his way to exculpate the two most prominent is indirect evidence of his involvement—not conclusive, yet it is suggestive.

Finally, it should be noted that F. Kozlov, whose power rose remarkably with Khrushchev's aid after 1952, discussed the need for political vigilance a few days before the doctor-affair was announced.[18] As already noted, the doctors were accused of having murdered Zhdanov and Shcherbakov, both of whom were linked with Khrushchev and Bulganin during the early post-Stalin years in politically significant lists of leaders.[19]

[18] *Kommunist,* No. 1 (January, 1953), pp. 46–58.
[19] See Rush, *The Rise of Khrushchev,* p. 17.

Whatever Stalin's intentions were regarding the leadership in the last months of his life, his sudden death prevented their realization. Those of his arrangements designed to strengthen his personal control of events were quickly reversed. The Party Presidium (formerly Politburo) and the Secretariat were reduced to their former size and ended up, for the most part, with their original personnel, who once more were listed in rank order.[20] Beria regained control of the political police, and his Ministry of Internal Affairs announced the exoneration of the accused doctors.[21]

The immediate problem created by Stalin's death was the disposition of the enormous powers he had exercised, so that government could continue. The triad he had established in the last years of his rule was a convenient transitional arrangement, but it did not provide a solution to the succession problem, since Stalin had failed to remove the counterweight to Malenkov's authority. Thus the two remaining members of the triad, Malenkov, the heir presumptive, and Khrushchev, the counter heir, now faced each other as opponents with no ruler to mediate between them.

Remarkably, a reorganization of the leadership was an-

[20] The announcement of this change hinted that the previous Presidium, which Stalin had set up, was unwieldy and its Bureau without authorization in the Party statute. His heirs saw "a need to have in the Central Committee of the CPSU, instead of two agencies of the Central Committee, the Presidium and the Bureau of the Presidium, one agency, the Presidium of the Central Committee of the CPSU, as set forth in the Party statute. In order to ensure more operative leadership, the Presidium shall consist of ten members and four candidates." *Pravda,* March 7, 1953.

[21] *Pravda,* April 4, 1953.

nounced the very day after Stalin's death.[22] An effort was made to establish the legitimacy of the new leadership by proclaiming it in the name of the Central Committee, the Council of Ministers, and the Presidium of the Supreme Soviet. While almost nothing is known of how this reorganization was actually decided upon, its effects are less obscure. Malenkov became head of the government, Beria was restored to control over the political police, Molotov to the conduct of foreign affairs. These three men were placed at the head of the rank-order listing of the Presidium. They spoke at Stalin's funeral, and during "the hundred days" preceding Beria's arrest their pronouncements on policy were often cited as programmatic. Malenkov, Beria, and Molotov constituted a triumvirate, however, only in a rather extended sense of the term. It is unlikely, for example, that they had agreed among themselves to exercise joint rule, or that the other leaders looked upon them as a ruling group. Molotov owed his place in it not to his own independent power or to the confidence he inspired in his fellow triumvirs, but rather to his prestige as an Old Bolshevik, a former head of the government, and a particularly close associate of Stalin's for many years. Beria's relation to Malenkov during this period has remained a puzzle. It can perhaps best be characterized as one of antagonistic cooperation. They probably arrived at agreement on the reorganization after negotiations based on their relative power and the need to take into account the interests and demands of the other principals.

22 Because of the rapid pace of the events announced and the obvious expediency of controlling the release of such information to the public, it cannot be excluded that Stalin was dead even before the stroke was publicized. Moreover, that Stalin did not meet a natural death can neither be affirmed nor denied with certainty.

Khrushchev's position was somewhat anomalous. On the one hand, he was not brought into the triumvirate. Nevertheless, in the initial reshuffle of top Party organs, Khrushchev and Malenkov emerged as the only Presidium members in the central Party Secretariat. This preserved the political relation between them that Stalin had created in his last years when he established the triad. Moreover, Khrushchev's special position in the Secretariat was foreshadowed by the initial joint decision: "To consider it necessary for Comrade N. S. Khrushchev to concentrate on work in the Central Committee of the CPSU and in this connection to relieve him of his duties as First Secretary of the Moscow Committee of the CPSU." [23]

Finally, Khrushchev improved his position in the rank-order listing of the Presidium, passing over Bulganin and Kaganovich. Malenkov clearly was *primus inter pares* in the triumvirate, whose existence he seemed to acknowledge by speaking of the three funeral speeches as authoritative statements of Soviet policy. Yet almost immediately there were signs that his special place in the triumvirate did not content him. For example, the day after Stalin's funeral (March 10) *Pravda* republished a three-year-old photograph from which most of the figures had been eliminated in order to show Malenkov standing alone with Mao Tse-tung and Stalin.

Malenkov's ambitions evoked opposition, and within a few days he was compelled to "request" release from his duties as Secretary of the Central Committee. As a result, the personal confrontation of Malenkov and Khrushchev, which began in Stalin's triadal succession arrangements and continued briefly after Stalin's death in the Central

[23] *Pravda,* March 7, 1953.

Secretariat, now took the form of an opposition based on competing institutions.

PERSONAL STRATEGIES

As we noted earlier, in winning the succession to Lenin, Stalin made the apparatus of full-time Party workers the sovereign institution in Soviet society. However, in the great purge of the mid-1930s it was reduced to an instrument of Stalin's absolute rule, though still the preeminent one, in an intricate system of institutional balances and controls that embraced the Party apparatus, the political police, the state bureaucracy, and the army. At Stalin's death, the complex system of institutional checks and balances that had maintained his absolute rule began to break up into its elements. The resulting institutional conflict was intensified as the leaders, in accordance with their personal strategies, recruited their forces for the portentous battles to come. Because these personal strategies illuminate the mechanics of power in a Soviet succession crisis, it is useful to consider them at some length.

The first strategy to be fully expressed in events was that of Beria. His one hundred days is not important in its own right, but for what it reveals of the political potential of various social groups during succession and for its indirect effect on subsequent developments.

Beria's strategy had several elements. The first and most essential was the recovery of control over the political police so that he could parry moves that had been initiated against him in Stalin's last months. He was restored to the Ministry of Internal Affairs (MVD) as part of a general arrangement whereby he, Molotov, Bulganin, and Mikoyan were made heads of the ministries with which they had long been associated. The next step was to place men on whom he could rely in the territorial offices of the Ministry. During the rest of his tenure Beria was engaged in purging unreliable political police officials in the Ukraine, Transcaucasia, the Baltic countries, and Central Asia. At the same time, it was desirable to remove something of the onus that was his as the political police chief. This was facilitated by the purge of the MVD and by the need to quash the doctor-affair, which enabled Beria to criticize the political police for its conduct during a time when he did not control it.

The most striking aspect of Beria's strategy was the effort to gain support from the so-called "national cadres," members of the various minority nationalities who had made successful careers in the Soviet system but still felt some allegiance to the peoples from whom they had sprung. Their response to Beria's scarcely veiled public appeals is not known to us. It is possible that in appealing for support to these groups in the borderland republics (the Ukraine, Transcaucasia, the Baltic countries, and Central Asia) Beria acted out of desperation, and that in addition he overestimated their political importance. Nevertheless, the fact that he tried to make the minority intelligentsia a basis for his political power suggests that their political potential may be greater than is commonly supposed.[24]

Control over the political police was necessary for his own protection, yet it inevitably posed a threat to Beria's colleagues, which in turn increased the danger to his own

24 *Pravda* accused Beria of "bourgeois-nationalist deviations" and of seeking to undermine the friendship of the peoples of the USSR (July 10, 1953).

position. Beria thus found himself moving in a vicious circle. His power seemingly rose rapidly throughout the one hundred days, only to culminate in his arrest at the end of June, 1953, by his Presidium colleagues. His fall initiated a struggle to benefit from his ill-fortune, whose course and outcome are suggested by two events: in early July, the case against Beria was presented to the Central Committee by Malenkov; five months later, when Beria was tried by a special tribunal, the prosecutor and at least three of the four judges were adherents of Khrushchev.

Malenkov's strategy from the outset was largely based on the state bureaucracy. He evidently supposed that the Party apparatus, and particularly its center, the Secretariat, could be weakened, and that the state bureaucracy, freed from constraint, could be made the dominant institution in Soviet society. He apparently justified his strategy doctrinally by arguing that Lenin intended state organs to have primacy over Party organs once the proletarian revolution was victorious. According to the theoretical journal of the Central Committee:

> Members of the anti-Party group departed from the Leninist understanding of the leading role of the Party in the system of the dictatorship of the proletariat. . . . Some of them . . . seeking to substantiate the [alleged] necessity of the primacy of state organs over Party, distorted the Leninist doctrine on the role of the Party after the victory of the proletarian revolution.[25]

To succeed, Malenkov's strategy required forceful and dangerous maneuvers. He had to strengthen the government apparatus, protecting it against encroachments by the provincial Party apparatus. This meant that through-

[25] *Kommunist,* No. 10 (July, 1957), p. 5.

out the Party hierarchy the Secretariat, particularly its First Secretary, had to be weakened and made to share its power more widely with the corresponding Party bureaus,[26] where the state bureaucracy was well represented. It was for this reason, no doubt, that Malenkov resurrected the phrase "collective leadership." Since provincial first secretaries were the strongest element in the Central Committee, Malenkov tried to keep that body without influence, just as in Stalin's day—at least until many more bureaucrats could be added to it. (In election speeches delivered in March, 1954, Malenkov was the only top leader who failed to mention the Central Committee.) To preserve the myth of Party sovereignty while in fact making the government supreme, Malenkov tried to dominate the Party Presidium so as to be able to promulgate policy in its name. To fashion Stalin's inert and diffuse bureaucracy into an effective instrument of rule, a strong government—that is, Council of Ministers—was required. In the very first hours after Stalin's death, Malenkov halved the number of ministries and increased the discretionary powers of their heads. By these means, the oversized bureaucracy was reduced and state authority was concentrated in the hands of a few powerful figures.

Despite some conservative features in Malenkov's reform strategy, it promised fundamental change. His decision to oppose the Party machine and its system of secretarial rule was crucial. It made him a supporter of the bureau in provincial Party organizations, where diverse social forces were represented; thus it opened the way to an incipient pluralism in Soviet politics. It made him a

[26] A bureau is the executive body of Party committees, corresponding to the Presidium of the Central Committee.

strong partisan of "liberalizing" policies that could enlist the support of the economic bureaucracy and perhaps deprive the Party of a key function: policing the system of priorities that favors heavy industry and armaments over consumption.

To justify his rule, Malenkov used two radically different means. As Stalin's heir presumptive he naturally identified himself with his predecessor during the first days of succession. He swore in his funeral speech to uphold Stalin's great principles, employing the clerical style that Stalin had affected at Lenin's funeral. Moreover, a photograph was altered, as noted earlier, to show Malenkov close by Stalin. This phase was quickly over, however, and Malenkov thereafter spoke with an authority based on his constitutional position as Chairman of the Council of Ministers.[27] From this position he addressed himself to the entire Soviet people, while Khrushchev spoke to the Party, and more especially to its inner core of full-time *apparatchiks*.

Khrushchev's personal strategy was from the outset closely modeled on Stalin's rise to power in the 1920s. As shown in the preceding chapter, Stalin began with a commanding position in the Party Secretariat and extended his control over the Party's administrative apparatus, including its elective machinery; this enabled him to make patronage appointments throughout the Party apparatus, even to positions which entailed membership in the Cen-

[27] It is not altogether clear why in 1924 the post of head of the government was assumed by Rykov rather than by one of the triumvirs. Apparently, it was thought presumptuous for a protagonist in the struggle over succession to assume Lenin's office, although Zinoviev did take over Lenin's role in delivering the report of the Central Committee to the Party Congress. See page 37, note 21.

tral Committee; by determining the membership of the Central Committee, Stalin in time gained control of its executive agency, the Politburo.

Khrushchev's choice of a similar road to power was largely determined by his personal circumstances at the time of Stalin's death and by his past career. From its beginning in the mid-1920s, his career had been in the Party apparatus; he had never held a post in the central government (the Council of Ministers), and in fact did not attain one until 1958, when he was to enter the government for the first time as its head. Moreover, with Malenkov's removal from the Secretariat in mid-March, Khrushchev became the sole Presidium member in that body, giving him a comparable advantage to that possessed by Stalin in the first phase of the Lenin succession. It was almost fated, therefore, that Khrushchev should try to follow in Stalin's footsteps.

Yet there were important differences in the circumstances of the two leaders when they launched their respective campaigns for supreme power. Stalin, in 1922, had still to make the Party apparatus the dominant institution in Soviet society; Khrushchev's problem, in 1953, was to restore the sovereignty that Stalin had taken from it more than a decade earlier. The lowly place of the Party apparatus in 1953 is suggested by Khrushchev's initial place in the leadership; although he was the ranking member of the Party apparatus, he was only the fifth-ranking member of the Presidium, after the triumvirate (Malenkov, Beria, and Molotov) and Voroshilov. In the central agencies of rule, Khrushchev's strategy required him to enhance the authority and the prestige of the Secretariat and its parent agency, the Central Committee, just as Malenkov's strategy required him to do this for the Council of Ministers and its parent agency, the Supreme Soviet. In August, Malenkov was still able to present his New Course program to the Supreme Soviet without getting prior approval from the Central Committee. September, 1953, was a turning point. At a meeting of the Central Committee Khrushchev largely succeeded in gaining control over agriculture for the Party apparatus, and he himself became the Party's spokesman on questions of agriculture. His special position within the Secretariat was now recognized by a new title, "First Secretary of the Central Committee," which was suggestive of Stalin's former title of "General Secretary of the Central Committee."

On becoming First Secretary Khrushchev still faced the problem of centralizing the territorial Party organizations under his personal control. He did not have to cope with great provincial satraps, as Stalin did in the mid-1920s. Yet his task presented some difficulty, since Khrushchev had worked chiefly in territorial organizations, and did not gain direct access to the central Party apparatus until three years before Stalin's death. Khrushchev was able to gain control over the Party machine largely by replacing leaders of the territorial Party organizations, where necessary, and installing his own adherents, many of them from the Ukraine where he had been their patron. Khrushchev also created a Russian Bureau of the Central Committee in order to strengthen his control over the Party apparatus in that key republic. As he became master of the Party machine, however, Khrushchev encouraged initiative from provincial leaders, and gave minority nationalities representation, mostly as candidate members, in the Presidium. On the other hand, Khrushchev successfully countered Malenkov's effort to further centralize economic administration in the government. He compelled Malenkov to split the ministries he had amalgamated, and brought about some devolution of economic administration to the republican governments. Finally, in mid-1957, he succeeded in dissolving almost all the economic ministries and conferring their *formal* powers on various agencies: the newly established provincial economic councils (*sovnarkhozi*), the state planning agency, and various central coordinating committees. In reality, however, at that time a decisive role in economic administration was conferred upon a not altogether willing Party apparatus.

In the provinces, just as Malenkov tried to increase the power and authority of the local bureau, Khrushchev attempted to strengthen the Secretariat. The balance between the two bodies necessarily depends in good measure upon the number of Secretaries, as appears from Khrushchev's speech at the XIX Party Congress in 1952: "In order to prevent the Secretariats' supplanting the Bureaus . . . the number of Secretaries should be reduced to three." On the pretext of strengthening Party leadership in agriculture Khrushchev began, in the fall of 1953, to increase the number of Secretaries on the lowest (raion) level beyond the statutory number of three, to four or even five. He gradually extended this practice upwards in the Party hierarchy to the oblast, the republic, and finally to the central Secretariat. In this way the Party apparatus came to dominate the policy-making as well as the administrative machinery. By mid-1957, after the purge of the anti-Party group, two-thirds of the Party Presidium consisted of Secretaries.

In the first years after Stalin's death, Khrushchev's power

grew more rapidly than his authority. He faced the problem of legitimizing this power, of establishing his right to rule. To achieve this, two ways are open to the protagonist for succession to the dictator. He can emulate his predecessor, proclaiming his former closeness to him and the similarity of their political views; or he can try to prove by some great feat that he possesses special qualities that justify his rule, what political sociologists call *charisma.* During the early years of succession, as he pursued Stalin's path to power, Khrushchev understandably chose to associate himself with Stalin and with his role in the Party's history.

This was the period when Khrushchev limited his appeals for support chiefly to the Party apparatus, while criticizing the economic bureaucracy, and for the most part neglected popular demands for a better material life. When controversy arose on a number of policy questions, Khrushchev's position was the one that Stalin might have approved. In agriculture, Malenkov favored increased reliance on experts, investment in the central areas, and intensive cultivation. Khrushchev wanted agriculture administered largely by the rural Party apparatus, and called for a crash program in the virgin and reclaimed lands to achieve a quick increase in grain production. As regards industry, a bitter dispute arose over Malenkov's efforts to improve supplies of consumer goods rapidly, at the cost of some retardation of the remarkable growth of heavy industry. Malenkov also sought to finance his consumer goods program by a moderate reduction in defense spending.

This led to a muted public controversy regarding the military threat posed by the Cold War. Malenkov seemed to believe that with the advent of thermonuclear weapons war became so dangerous to both sides that it required, and at the same time made possible, a negotiated settlement of the Cold War. This view was challenged in 1954 and 1955 by the Khrushchev faction, which stressed instead that the new weapons increased the danger of a surprise attack on the USSR. It called for increased defense spending and vigorous conduct of the Cold War.

The strategies of the two protagonists, and of the loose factions that supported them in the leadership, were applied in ways that are relatively clear in outline, though not always in detail. Malenkov was supported by the leading economic administrators whom he had raised to the Presidium, Saburov and Pervukhin, as well as by Mikoyan on certain issues, and he was backed by numerous figures in the Council of Ministers. Khrushchev was supported at first by the men whom Stalin had raised to eminence in the 1920s: Molotov, Kaganovich, and Voroshilov, as well as by Bulganin, the Minister of Defense. They feared Malenkov because of his bid to seize dictatorial power in the first days after Stalin died, and were also concerned at his subsequent effort to establish a new course in foreign and domestic policy. They relied on Khrushchev to organize the necessary support to defeat Malenkov, just as Zinoviev and Kamenev had relied on Stalin to help them defeat Trotsky.

As soon as this faction succeeded in defeating Malenkov and demoting him (February, 1955), the ties holding it together began to unravel. Some of Khrushchev's erstwhile allies now attempted to strengthen the Council of Ministers (of which Khrushchev was not a member) as the chief policy-making body and to limit Khrushchev's powers as

First Secretary.[28] Their first efforts, in the spring of 1955, met early defeat when Khrushchev succeeded, in July, in bringing his supporters into the Party Presidium and into a newly strengthened Secretariat.

Since Khrushchev's bid for power was based on the Party apparatus and was patterned on Stalin's use of it to make himself the supreme leader, it was natural that Khrushchev, in the developing controversy over Stalin, should take his part. Yet there was a certain ambiguity in Khrushchev's relation to Stalin, as there had been in Stalin's relation to the Party apparatus. After elevating the Party apparatus, Stalin had turned against it in the 1930s, subjecting it to a terrible blood purge and depriving it of sovereignty. Khrushchev's intention of making the Party apparatus the sovereign institution once more committed him to altering the system that Stalin had handed down when he died. Moreover, his choice of Stalin's way to power imposed constraints which he increasingly felt to be restrictive. After defending Stalin, Khrushchev found it expedient, at a critical point in the succession struggle, to abandon this role and to become Stalin's accuser. This he did in the speech to the XX Party Congress.

By assuming the role of the destroyer of the Stalin myth and the reformer of Stalin's institutional heritage, Khrushchev established a new basis for his claim to rule. He be-

[28] See, for example, the article by the Old Bolshevik and survivor of the great purge, G. I. Petrovsky, in *Pravda,* April 20, 1955. "Once a week and sometimes twice a week the Council of People's Commissars met under the chairmanship of Lenin. At meetings of the Council of People's Commissars all the important problems of the first steps of social construction and the organization of Soviet power in the center and locally were considered. Questions were decided concerning liquidation of all bourgeois institutions. The first steps of socialist production and trade were outlined here."

came the doer of great deeds, not the follower of his predecessor. Khrushchev now strove to associate himself with Lenin, the doer of the greatest deeds.

The year following the XX Party Congress was filled with difficulties and complications for Khrushchev in his bid for dictatorial power. His sudden attack on Stalin caused unrest throughout the Soviet bloc, as well as resistance in Poland and bloody revolt in Hungary. Inside the USSR, Khrushchev had to retain the allegiance of the Party apparatus, while at the same time extending his appeal to a wider public in order to gain popular support for his reform program and to undermine the authority of his colleagues.[29] Once again state bodies were used to oppose him. However, Khrushchev counterattacked in the Central Committee, in February, 1957, and placed his Presidium opponents in jeopardy of losing their institutional bases of support in the economic ministries. They attempted once more, as in 1955, to restrict his power, but this time with a boldness and an urgency that were born of desperation. Relying on his control over the Central Committee and its apparatus, Khrushchev defeated their attempt to pare his power.[30] With a single stroke he destroyed the opposition.

Stalin's despotic power, which had been distributed at his death, and subsequently redistributed again and again in forms that proved to be unstable, had now found a

[29] In speeches delivered before large audiences in the spring of 1957, Khrushchev aired a number of proposals that were still being considered by the Presidium.

[30] While it has generally been assumed in the West that the so-called "anti-Party group" attempted to remove Khrushchev as First Secretary in June, 1957, this has never been asserted in the Soviet press. It is contradicted by the testimony of those of its members who have been allowed to express themselves publicly.

proper equilibrium. The Stalin succession crisis was resolved. Much of Stalin's former power was in Khrushchev's hands, but enough remained outside to warrant calling this new mode of rule Khrushchev's limited dictatorship. Some months after he had purged his opponents, in March, 1958, Khrushchev made himself head of the government, and thus placed a seal of formal legitimacy on his rule.

Khrushchev had begun to moderate his position on policy matters as soon as he had defeated Malenkov, his chief rival, and had won control over the Party apparatus. As early as February, 1955, his measures began to resemble in some respects those Malenkov had advocated. Nevertheless, important differences remained. Khrushchev sought a *détente* with the West, yet he seemed less committed than Malenkov had been to negotiating outstanding differences, and more interested in extending Communist influence throughout the world. His subsequent efforts, after 1960, to keep down military spending were combined with a strategy of deceiving the West regarding Soviet military power and of using this deception as the basis for an offensive political strategy. In domestic politics, Khrushchev gave increased priority to satisfying the great hunger for consumer goods, but not until September, 1964, a few weeks before his ouster, did he commit himself, as Malenkov had, to an extended slowdown in the rate of growth of producer goods. Just as Stalin, in "taking over" Trotsky's economic program in 1928, transformed it almost beyond recognition, so Khrushchev, in so far as he was influenced by Malenkov's views, made them distinctively his own in execution.

Stalin's effort to preserve his system intact had failed, as it was probably fated to from the start. It could have been preserved in its disregard of the people—of their longing for a better material life and an end to the terror—only if the dead Stalin were replaceable by a living one. But this was impossible: not only was Stalin unique, but his heirs were determined not to suffer another Stalin. As we have said, the Stalin succession was resolved by the establishment of a *limited* dictatorship. Yet, while Stalin's effort to confine his successors to the orthodoxy he had laid down met with failure, it was only a partial failure. Khrushchev's object was reform and renovation, not destruction. Basic features of Stalin's system persisted, as did Khrushchev's ambivalent relation to Stalin and his heritage.

IV: Character of Soviet Succession Crises

From the accounts just given it is evident that when the USSR has faced the succession problem, it has experienced a crisis. By "crisis" I do not mean that the system was on the brink of dissolution but only that the USSR had reached a turning point, a state of affairs in which a decisive change could occur. In this dictionary sense of the term it seems hardly questionable that the Soviet Union experienced a crisis after Lenin's mortal illness and again after Stalin's death. The question naturally arises whether succession in the USSR inevitably produces a crisis, so that a third one will follow Khrushchev's overthrow.

INEVITABILITY OF SUCCESSION CRISES

A succession crisis *is* to be expected. This conclusion is not simply grounded in history; the nature of the Soviet political system appears to make such crises inevitable.[1] There are two reasons why this is so. First, in the Soviet

[1] For an historical treatment of succession in the USSR, see the article by Bohdan R. Bociurkiw, "The Problem of Succession in the Soviet Political System: The Case of Khrushchev," in *The Canadian Journal of Economics and Political Science,* XXVI (November, 1960), 575–91.

system, there is no established decision-making center whose authority is recognized at all times. Second, for this reason, and for others to be cited, no orderly method of succession has been or is likely to be devised.

To the question of where decisive authority or internal sovereignty resides, a formal answer can, of course, be found in the Party statute and in the state constitution. But these documents are not the ultimate authority in the Soviet system, and their provisions have often been disregarded. Does the supreme authority reside in the government's Council of Ministers or in organs of the Party? If the Party is sovereign, which of its bodies has the power of decision—the Presidium or the Secretariat? Or is it the Central Committee, which meets briefly every few months? Or the Party Congress, which meets every few years? It is apparent from our accounts of the Lenin and Stalin successions that Soviet history gives no single answer; it has been different at different times. The question of supreme authority is the fundamental issue of Soviet politics and has been fought over by its chief figures. Uncertainty as to the decisive authority may ultimately imperil the regime, but only in the absence of an established ruler or dictator —that is, during a succession crisis—is the problem acute.

There is a paradox here. The Soviet system has been most stable until now when it has had a dictator, yet dictatorial authority inheres in no office or title. It is unprovided for in the fundamental laws of Party and state, which establish collective organs of leadership without exception. As a result there is no rule for establishing the legitimacy of the dictator. While Lenin ruled, this problem did not arise. He ruled the Party because he was its founder, and he governed the state because he was the source of the revolution that created it. But by what right did his successors rule? Stalin's rule had no legitimate basis in the state constitution, inasmuch as Stalin ruled for more than a decade before he entered the government; it had no basis in the Party statute, which did not even mention his post of General Secretary of the Central Committee, and of course said nothing of a *vozhd,* or leader of the Party. Stalin sought to make the cult of Lenin one source of the legitimacy of his rule, but this only made his rule the more questionable since Lenin had secretly denounced him. Khrushchev's rule also suffered from a radical defect, for he could claim no personal ties with Lenin, and he had finally disavowed Stalin as a source of legitimacy. Both Khrushchev and Stalin tried to base their authority on the Central Committee, as in the formula: "the Central Committee, headed by Khrushchev [Stalin]." Yet this formula does not provide a principle of legitimacy, since there is nowhere provision for a head of the Central Committee: an individual can achieve this eminence only by making himself its master, but to do this is to base legitimacy on illegality, which is at best a doubtful foundation. In last analysis, the chief sanction for the dictator's rule in the Soviet system is the fact that he exercises it, and has placed it beyond the challenge of legitimate political activity. While this sanction may suffice for the incumbent, it has the defect that it provides no principle for establishing the legitimacy of a successor until he too has placed his rule beyond challenge by customary political means.

Conceivably, election to some special office might be a means of authorizing dictatorial power during a crisis. But which office? Senior Secretary of the Central Committee might seem suitable. But Lenin was never a Secretary, and both Stalin and Khrushchev headed the Secretariat for several years without being accorded recognition as the personal ruler.[2] The post of Senior Secretary is rightly coveted for the advantage it gives in the struggle for the succession. But mere occupancy of the post does not command obedience. The office of Senior Secretary is far less valuable for the authority it confers than for the opportunity it affords the incumbent to aggrandize power.

Although no office now exists that confers dictatorial authority, is this lack not remediable? Could the ruler not proclaim, for example, that his powers inhere jointly in the offices of Senior Secretary and Chairman of the Council of Ministers, and declare that when these posts fall vacant the Central Committee is to meet to elect a single successor to both posts? To institutionalize personal dictatorship in this way would run counter to Party traditions. But the decisive objection to such a scheme is that it requires the members of the Central Committee (or whatever body might be designated) to give themselves up to a new master of their own choosing at the very time when the ruler's demise, political or physical, has provided them with a moment of enhanced power and relative freedom. This does not seem an effective device for averting a succession crisis.

One final and seemingly simple solution remains to be considered. Could the ruler not arrange the succession by surrendering full power to the man of his choice? The act of transfer would still be a complicated one; after attempting it the ruler could find that although he no longer

[2] Stalin's title of General Secretary was grander than Khrushchev's of First Secretary, but it probably has been discredited along with Stalin, who alone bore it.

possessed his former power, his designated heir had not acquired it. Even if the heir did acquire supreme power, he might prove unacceptable to his former peers, or incapable of exercising the vast powers that had been handed him.

If the heir did succeed to his predecessor's powers and was able to maintain his rule, the problem of succession would have been solved. Even so, the former ruler might have strong reason to regret what he had done. He might be compelled to witness the discarding of his favorite policies and lieutenants, along with his whole program for improving Soviet society. His advice on these and other matters might not only be disregarded, but resented. Regardless of his intention, he would inevitably pose a threat to the new ruler, as a potential center of opposition. At the same time, having given up his dictatorial power, the old ruler would be at the mercy of the new. Despite these perils, which are sure to be anticipated, a Soviet dictator conceivably might appear who was willing to perform this selfless and hazardous act. Its attraction would perhaps be greatest in the very special situation of a dictator who secretly suffered from a fatal disease. It is a solution that cannot be ruled out, although the likelihood of its occurring seems sufficiently small to warrant disregarding it in what follows.

Granted that the ruler is unlikely to surrender willingly the plenitude of his power to an heir, might he not designate a successor and provide him with sufficient power to make good his claim at the decisive moment when the ruler is no longer present to impose his will? (Orderly transfer of power to a collective is a possible, but doubtful, solution, which is discussed later.) Arranging this is an extremely hazardous undertaking. If the ruler delegates wide powers to a lieutenant, he may invite attempts to seize the remainder. Moreover, once the ruler's choice of a successor is known, his entourage may pay court to the favorite rather than to himself; alternatively, they may concentrate their fire on the heir presumptive, who endangers their present power and threatens to become their next master.

The ruler's dilemma is not without a solution or at least the promise of one. The power of the heir presumptive can be circumscribed by that of others. Perhaps the chief danger in this arrangement is that the heir may reach an accommodation with some of his rivals. This danger may be reduced, though not eliminated, by concentrating substantial power in the hands of a single rival, thus forming a triad made up of the personal ruler, whose power is much greater than that of the other members; his heir presumptive; and the rival, who may be termed the counter heir. As we have seen, this was basically Stalin's arrangement for the succession in his last years.

In choosing an heir, the ruler is of course limited to the men at hand. Even if talented leaders are among them, the choice is difficult. If the ruler chooses an able and assertive lieutenant and gives him too little power, that lieutenant will be unable to make himself ruler at the moment of succession. If the ruler tries to obviate this difficulty, however, by selflessly granting the heir presumptive large powers, the succession may be initiated by his own overthrow, which is not conducive to an orderly succession. A mediocre heir presumptive, on the other hand, could safely be granted large powers, but they probably would still be insufficient to assure him the succession.

Timing is an important part of the difficulty in sharing power with the heir presumptive. The ruler may plan to do so "at the right moment," but that moment is hard to find. When things are going badly, the ruler is reluctant to rely on his heirs to improve matters, and if they begin to go well he sees little reason for change.

The heir presumptive, for his part, faces an elaborate series of obstacles, the greatest of which is encountered at the decisive moment of succession. The power and authority that he has been granted may prove insufficient to make him ruler, yet, because he was favored by the predecessor and given an advantage over the others, he is a marked man. There is nothing so dangerous as to be an heir presumptive with insufficient authority.

To sum up: Designation is not a principle of legitimacy in the Soviet system, for the dictator's fiat may be disregarded. As we have seen, neither Stalin nor Lenin was able to effectuate his will after his lifetime. Moreover, an attempt to establish machinery for ensuring the succession of the chosen heir can lead to the ruler's own overthrow. In the absence of any principle of legitimacy, the means available to the ruler for arranging the succession seem to be inadequate.

In the USSR, then, the new ruler evidently comes to his office not by an orderly transfer of authority but by arrogating power to himself. As a result, for a time, at least, the functions normally performed by the ruler go undone. Moreover, the process by which this state of affairs can be rectified, namely, the concentration of great power in the person of the successor, is disruptive. It is these two consequences of the failure to provide for succession that produce political crisis in the Soviet system.

The chief function performed by the ruler in the Soviet system is to provide authoritative decisions. He constitutes a recognized and accepted source for decisions on the most important questions—a source which does not otherwise exist. Under his rule personal and group rivalries occur and may, in fact, be highly intense, but the issues of policy and preferment over which battles rage ultimately come to him to be resolved. His capacity to resolve them, if necessary by compromising his own views, prevents contention among other officials from getting out of hand. Once he has decided, the battle must subside, unless the losing group is prepared to challenge the ruler himself. In fact, only while he is able to prevent such challenges, or put them down if they occur, does he rule as dictator. By being the ultimate source of decision, the dictator is able to arbitrate disputes, thereby setting important limits to legitimate political activity and giving stability to the leadership.

The significance of this arbitral function, which is crucial in any political system, is especially so in the USSR where the power of the state over society is so great. In the absence of a ruler not only are the many issues of policy more difficult to resolve, but a new and qualitatively different issue becomes a subject of contention, the question, who is to decide? This is a fundamental issue of politics, and one difficult to settle by compromise. *The prolonged absence of a dictator need not mean the collapse of the Soviet system, but it might entail loss by the state of some of its great powers in circumstances where it was unable to exercise them effectively.* Moreover, if faced with critical issues involving preservation of the regime's character, such an unstable leadership would find it increasingly difficult to cope with them.

There are other functions of the ruler the nonperformance of which might be seriously disruptive. As dictator, he authenticates doctrine and inaugurates ideological change. He unifies in his person ideology, policy, and organization, and therefore confers upon policy both its sacred character and the means of its implementation. Yet, in last analysis, it is his capacity to make authoritative decisions, and in particular to decide between groupings, that makes the ruler indispensable over the long run if the Soviet system is to preserve its historical character. (In the very long run, of course, some new institution may be devised to perform this function.)

The process whereby a dictator is restored to the system tends to be disruptive, first, because it is illicit, and, second, because so much is at stake. Contenders for the succession rely upon informal groupings of peers and followers who are like-minded or share common political or personal interests. The activities of these groupings, or factions, are necessarily conducted in a conspiratorial atmosphere since the Party statute expressly prohibits "attempts to form factional groupings destructive of Party unity" (article 27). A Soviet ruler ordinarily tolerates factional activity, which is everywhere the stuff of politics, and even fosters it for his own ends; only if there is special reason will he destroy a faction and punish its chief members. (A shocking instance of this was Stalin's blood purge of the Leningrad faction, 1948–1950.) In a succession struggle, however, the stakes of factional activity are far greater than under a dictator. Rivals for the succession suppose their opponent incapable of the prudent exercise of such vast powers, which are perhaps greater than any other man on earth possesses; moreover they fear for themselves should he acquire them. Thus, as one contender gains an advantage, there is a tendency for the others to combine against him.

A victor in this struggle will be virtually dictator, yet he will feel threatened by the defeated. To consolidate his newly won power, he is inclined to condemn his opponents as factionalists and enemies of the Party. Thus the contending factions in a succession crisis are subject to severe statutory sanctions. The mere threat to apply specific sanctions may often suffice to compel a defeated faction to confess to transgressions of which the victorious faction is no less guilty. For example, according to the Central Committee's resolution in 1957 "on the anti-Party group": "when members of the C.C. Plenum unanimously demanded the expulsion of the members of the group from the C.C. and *their exclusion from the Party,* they acknowledged the existence of a conspiracy and the harmfulness of their anti-Party activity, and promised to submit to decisions of the Party."[3] Apparently it was the threat of expulsion from the Party, which would have prepared the way for criminal proceedings, that compelled key members of the defeated faction to confess that they had violated the Party's statutes. That they feared worse than expulsion was asserted by Khrushchev himself:

> When the anti-Party group was smashed, its participants expected that they would be treated in the same way they had dealt with people at the time of the cult of the individual, and in the way they hoped to deal with those who favored the restoration of Leninist norms of Party life.[4]

[3] *KPSS v resoliutsiiakh i resheniiakh* (The CPSU in Resolutions and Decisions) (Moscow, Gospolitizdat, 1960), IV, 276. Emphasis added.

[4] *Pravda,* October 27, 1961.

Khrushchev's implicit contention that the defeated group intended to engage in a blood purge of its opponents may be malicious; but his willingness to make such a charge implies a belief that even after the exposure of Stalin's crimes at the XX Congress, which was supposed to make their repetition impossible, it is still credible to many in the Soviet Union that the victors in a succession crisis would try to destroy the defeated.

It seems unlikely that the contestants in a future succession will altogether rule out the possibility of suffering severe sanctions for their participation. But even the assurance that their lives would not be forfeit need not lessen the acuteness of the struggle. After all, it was not because of concern for their lives that Stalin's Old Bolshevik rivals persisted in opposing him. Assurance that the penalty for defeat would not be death might even embolden the contenders to continue and intensify the struggle, so long as there were any hope of winning it. They would hope thereby to save their careers and, as they might believe, their country and its Revolution.

To conclude: In the USSR the ruler evidently cannot inherit authority but must win it, and it is difficult to see how such vast powers can be seized against the certain opposition of rivals without producing a political crisis. Its depth and effects, however, are variable, according to the scope and intensity of the struggle and the manner of its resolution.

CHARACTER OF THE SUCCESSION CRISIS

Succession is initiated by the political or physical demise of the ruler. The circumstances in which this event occurs may significantly affect the course of succession, yet even the ruler who attempts to arrange his succession cannot know with confidence what these circumstances will be.

The ruler may be struck with an incapacitating illness that finally leaves him infirm and ineffectual, as Lenin was; his life may be cut off sharply and unexpectedly, as Stalin's was; or his faculties may decline with age, which, according to the Central Committee, is what happened to Khrushchev. The ruler's demise may be a political rather than a physical event as when he is removed in a palace revolt, as Khrushchev was *in fact,* in which case his person and policies immediately become a central issue in the succession. The ruler may be assassinated, either by an opponent of the regime, as Lenin almost was in August, 1918, or as part of some Kremlin plot, as Stalin's deputy, Sergei Kirov, was in 1934.

The full consequences of an assassination of the dictator, were it to occur, are hard to imagine. In the short term the leaders would be inclined to close themselves off from the public and to increase the powers of the political police. They would have a heightened sense of their common interest as against the interests and aspirations of the technical intelligentsia and intellectuals, and the demands of the unprivileged masses of the people. The succession struggle might not lose anything of its intensity, but the contending leaders would be more strongly motivated to prevent its spread into the wider arena of Soviet society. As a result, the cause of reform in the USSR would probably suffer. In tsarist Russia there was a strong tradition of political assassination in a part of the revolutionary movement, which persisted into the Bolshevik period. It is extremely doubtful, however, that an assassination could be carried out by a revolutionary group in the USSR today.

However it begins, the succession crisis is at the outset largely colored by the personal rivalry of the most ambitious of the former ruler's heirs. In their efforts to inherit his power, they are compelled to maneuver and compromise, forming factions in the top leadership according to the shifting calculation of personal interest and political principle. Such factions, as we noted earlier, also pervade politics under the unchallenged rule of the dictator. At that time their object is to influence the dictator, to share patronage, and to protect their members. In a succession crisis, however, there is no unchallenged authority to arbitrate differences and to limit the scope of factional activity, which is considerably intensified and develops according to a new logic. The organizational forms of a faction may become more elaborate and extensive, possibly embracing persons in the middle or lower echelons. Factions may acquire influence in particular organs of the press, where they can make known their special views on key questions of policy, and perhaps even publicize incipient platforms of related policies. Such developments occurred in the 1920s, after Lenin became ill, and again, although with significant differences, after Stalin died in 1953.

A faction's strength is reflected in its representation in the regime's top organs, but the substance of that strength is the faction's influence in institutions and social groups. There are four chief sources of political power in the Soviet Union.

1. *The institutions of dictatorship.* During a period of succession struggle these serve the contending factions as

levers of power. The chief of these institutions is the Party apparatus (or Party machine), whose center is the Secretariat of the Central Committee. The other major institutions are (or have been): the state bureaucracy, the system of productive enterprises, the army, and the political police. Finally, there are subsidiary bodies, sometimes called the Party's "transmission belts," which could play an important role in future crises: the state system of Soviets, or formal legislative bodies, the trade union association, intellectuals' organizations (such as the Writers' Union), the Young Communist League (Komsomol), and others.

2. *Territorial bases of power.* An institution may not be wholly subject to a particular faction, but its parts may be controlled by leaders of a large city or a Union-republic. Such territorial bases played a key role in the first years of the Lenin succession crisis and were crucially important for at least a short period after Stalin's death.

3. *Professional groups.* Because of their functional importance in the working of the system, technically trained persons have an important political potential, although they are able to realize it only through association with particular institutions. Actually, professional persons tend to concentrate in particular institutions and in time form an allegiance to the institution that has shaped their career and on which the realization of their ambitions may depend. While that allegiance is compatible with abstract loyalty to the *Party,* it can become the basis for antagonism to the *Party machine.* One major professional group comprises economic technicians, who are mostly to be found in productive enterprises or in economic bodies, although Khrushchev has significantly increased their numbers in the Party apparatus. It remains to be seen

whether that body will succeed in assimilating them politically.

4. *Personal influence.* The prestige, personal associations, and popular following of a leader may cut across institutional, territorial, and professional lines. These personal assets become sources of factional power to the extent that they can be made to serve the faction's interests.

Even in the phase of stable dictatorship, these sources of political power are in a state of considerable tension; in a succession crisis, tension readily becomes acute conflict. The leaders who manipulate these bases of power mean to limit this conflict, to keep them mere agencies of dictatorship and passive objects of factional politics; but in such circumstances these bodies can acquire a life and movement of their own.

There are several ways in which this can come about. For example, a faction that has lost a battle may be tempted to seek support within organizations controlled by its opponents; or it may support the authority and interests of functionaries in organizations that it already controls in order to increase their potency as factional instruments. In either case, the result may be to make the faction dependent on groups that formerly were excluded from higher politics. Having been drawn into the higher politics of the Soviet regime, these groups acquire a voice in it. An instance of this is the role played by army leaders in the Stalin succession crisis: though not decisive, it significantly affected developments, and in turn won for the army some temporary autonomy. In this fashion, major institutions and territorial organizations may come to be altered and the balance among them upset. If the succession struggle acquires this new dimension, the regime may be modified in important ways.

Finally, if the crisis cannot be resolved within this enlarged arena, a weakened faction may seek to redress the balance by appealing to the passions and interests of broad groups in Soviet society. Thus Beria instigated criticism of "great-power chauvinism" (i.e., Russian nationalism) in the spring of 1953 in a desperate effort to gain the support of the political leaders and intelligentsia of the national minorities. Under comparable circumstances in 1926 and 1927, the Left Opposition appealed to Party cells of workers against Stalin's close-knit Party machine. This reaching out towards "the Party masses" adds a further dimension to the struggle and under certain circumstances might seriously weaken the regime or lead to its transformation.

The duration of the succession struggle is not a primary factor but is important chiefly as it affects the intensity of the struggle. A brief crisis can produce a great effect, but a prolonged crisis is much more likely to bring about the political activation of potentially powerful forces in Soviet society. Of the two succession crises the regime has known, the one after Lenin lasted roughly eight years, from his incapacitating illness in 1922 until roughly 1930, and the one after Stalin only four years, from 1953 to 1957. As is apparent from our accounts of the two crises, their prolongation produced a temporary increase in the number and variety of those who were drawn into higher politics as auxiliaries of the protagonists; but such tendencies were halted and then reversed each time by the most powerful contender, after he had consolidated his power and thereby resolved the crisis.

EFFECT OF SUCCESSION ON THE REGIME

The decisive question in the succession crisis is the manner of its resolution. More particularly, the position of the Party apparatus in the newly stabilized regime provides a rough test of whether the succession crisis has changed the character of the system. If the *apparat,* or Party machine, exercises hegemony over the other institutions of dictatorship and over Soviet society, then the regime almost certainly remains totalitarian.[5] The duration, the scope, and the intensity of the succession crisis work their effects on the character of the Soviet regime in good measure through their influence on this question. If the crisis is brief and easily resolved, the hegemony of the Party machine seems assured. If it is long and intense, and if important social groups become engaged in the higher politics of the USSR, then its hegemony may be endangered and its authority conceivably may be overthrown.

What is the Party machine, and why is its position so crucial in the Soviet system? The Party *apparat* is made up of the Party's permanent staff, its paid officials,[6] whose number has been very roughly estimated at around a quarter-

[5] By a totalitarian regime I mean, briefly, a political system in which a self-chosen elite attempts to transform the entire society over which it rules according to the prescriptions of a systematic doctrine, or ideology. From this attempt there follows a number of characteristic features, such as: mass indoctrination of the population in an exoteric version of the ideology; suppression of dissident opinion; a systematic effort to reduce the influence of traditional institutions; prohibition of voluntary associations that are unauthorized by the state; basic hostility to other political systems; and so forth.

[6] A new and anomalous category, "the nonstaff" Party functionary, has been created in recent years, but its members hold their principal position in, and draw their personal income from, an institution other than the machine.

million.[7] It must be distinguished from the Party's membership as a whole, which is perhaps forty times as large. It must further be distinguished from the system of territorial committees and their executive agencies, the bureaus, which exercise *de jure* authority at the various levels of the Party hierarchy, reaching at its summit to the Central Committee and its Presidium. *Apparatchiks* are a minority in these higher Party bodies, which include economic administrators, government officials, military officers, political police officials, and newspaper editors. Yet the power position of the Party machine is a crucial question in Soviet politics because it appears to be the main source of totalitarianism.

The Party machine is committed to fashioning Soviet institutions and Soviet man in accordance with an ideal, however undelineated, that permanently threatens the habits and customs of the people at large. As custodian of the holy writings of Marx and Lenin, it embodies most of what remains of the revolutionary spirit in the Soviet regime. It is responsible for indoctrinating a population acknowledged to be lacking in enthusiasm for the official ideology. Since its political character was largely formed in the Bolshevist image, the Party machine values control, power, and the future, as opposed to spontaneity, enjoyment, and the present. It sets the goals of economic activity and enforces the system of priorities that favors the more rapid growth of industrial and military power than of consumer goods.

The Soviet people accept the regime that governs them,

[7] Leonard Schapiro, *The Communist Party of the Soviet Union* (New York, Random House, 1960), pp. 524–25, 572–73.

for they see no alternative. Yet they do not fully share the Party's fundamental goals, which involve the continuing revolutionary transformation of Soviet society; nor are they committed to its ultimate objective, a worldwide Communist system. This gives rise to a certain tension, or "contradiction," between the Party machine and the populace. It is a contradiction that even the continuing abatement of the terror of Stalin's time and progressive improvement of the material conditions of life are unlikely to remove.

Reservations of various kinds about the Party machine's goals are also evident in the institutions controlled by the Party. These reservations seem especially strong among the economic managers and the state bureaucracy. Their primary professional concerns include the obvious functions of production, technology, labor discipline, and finance. In addition, they are deeply engaged in the politics of planning. Though they have conflicting interests, members of the bureaucratic elite also share important goals. One is to reduce the ambitious pace of economic development that strains Soviet resources to the limit. Another is to improve the forms and methods of administration and perhaps to establish a more rational price system. Perhaps most important, the bureaucracy wants to lessen arbitrary interference by the full-time members of the Party machine.

The opposition between the interests and goals of functionaries in the state bureaucracy and those in the Party machine, in so far as it finds institutional expression, is basic. State officials can be divided for convenience into "bureaucrats" and "specialists," although particular officials may have something of both in their character. In so far as they are specialists, state officials pride themselves on their training and experience and tend to place greater reliance on science and technology in solving problems than on ideology and a Leninist (or Bolshevik) style of leadership. In so far as they are bureaucrats, state officials prefer to be governed by fixed rules, to "go through channels"; they oppose intervention from the outside. They favor bureaucratic rationality: orderly procedure, routine, efficiency. They are inclined to disregard problems that are not pressing, and to seek a stereotyped solution for problems that cannot be disregarded. Regularity is their watchword. In their personal careers, Soviet bureaucrats, like bureaucrats everywhere, seem to favor stability, security, regular advancement, and greater material rewards.

While the Party machine also displays strong bureaucratic tendencies, it has succumbed to them less than state officialdom. It puts ideology and enthusiasm above both scientific and bureaucratic rationality. Typically, the Party sets new tasks, mobilizes opinion, shifts cadres; it locates difficulties, fixes responsibility for mistakes, and ensures that non-Party institutions carry out Party orders. Its preferred activity is the "crash" program. By its militant spirit and organization the Party made the October Revolution, won the civil war, and carried out Stalin's social revolution "from above."

The Party official and the economic executive are not separate breeds. They are frequently shifted from one bureaucracy to the other, particularly at the lowest and highest levels. Yet officials in the USSR tend to identify their personal fortunes with the political fortunes of the bureaucracy that has largely formed their political ideas, policy preferences, and personal skills. Khrushchev has himself alluded to the special mentality of the economic administrator, although in this case he opposed the central administrator to the provincial official:

The Central Committee of the CPSU has had to correct and rebuke those leaders who, from force of habit, still tend towards bureaucractic methods of management. Facts have been cited at this conference about certain chairmen of State committees who wanted to assume responsibility for various enterprises which are under the jurisdiction of the *sovnarkhozes.* This is an old disease caused by the fact that old Ministers head certain State committees. They are good Ministers, but even good Ministers are not immune from bad inclinations.[8]

The extent to which the Party and government bureaucracies remained separate under Stalin is suggested by the fact that more than half of the leading Party officials in his time had held no government post, and one-third of the leading government officials had never served in the Party machine. This can be inferred from the factual findings of T. H. Rigby.[9] Of 36 republic Party secretaries whose previous careers were known to Rigby, 20 had not held government posts. This was also true in the following cases: 38 of 82 territorial and regional Party secretaries; 29 of 43 city Party secretaries; 86 of 138 district Party secretaries. By the same token, as Rigby emphasizes, these figures also show that interchange of personnel between the two bureaucracies was practiced extensively. Significantly, it was easier to rise in the Party apparatus without having served in the administrative bureaucracy (more than half the Party leaders studied by Rigby had no experience in government) than to rise in the bureaucracy without having served in the machine (only one-third). From this it

[8] *Pravda,* April 26, 1963.

[9] "The Selection of Leading Personnel in the Soviet State and Communist Party," a doctoral thesis submitted at the University of London in 1954 (table on p. 184).

appears that even under Stalin the Party apparatus was a surer road to success than the bureaucracy.

The tendency of officials to become specialists in either Party work or administration has gone sufficiently far that top leaders openly speak of Party work as a profession. According to Frol Kozlov: "That full-time functionaries play an important role in the life of the Party is common knowledge. As we approach Communism, however, Party work, becoming less and less of a profession, will assume the nature of a voluntary social obligation." [10]

Possessing contrasting traits and performing overlapping functions, the state and the Party bureaucracies have naturally tended to oppose each other. Their mutual opposition played a role in the Lenin succession, but it was limited by the low prestige of the non-Communist specialist and the suspicion he was under among Communists. As we have seen, however, the opposition of the two bureaucracies was central in the Stalin succession. What conclusions can be drawn from the bureaucratic elite's fortunes in this struggle? Economic administrators were deeply involved in the Stalin succession crisis. Evidence of their potential political strength is implicit in the actions of both Malenkov, who made the bureaucratic elite his main power base, and Khrushchev, who took drastic action to eradicate its influence in Moscow. Indeed, the bureaucratic elite proved itself an autonomous political force, and not merely an instrument of factional intrigue, by maintaining the struggle with the Party machine long after its principal leader had lost his position as head of the government. Yet the completeness of its defeat and the relative ease with which this was accomplished suggest

[10] F. R. Kozlov, "CPSU—The Party of the Entire People," *World Marxist Review,* Vol. V, No. 6 (June, 1962), p. 7.

that its potentialities at Stalin's death were less than Malenkov had supposed. The outcome, however, provides no simple measure of the relative strength of the Party and state bureaucracies. In the highly fluid situation after Stalin died, other things had their effect: chance, the strategies and personal qualities of the contenders, and the role of the political police are only three among them.

The role of the bureaucratic elite in the massive and intricate Soviet economy remains crucial. In the post-Stalin years the economic bureaucracy was repeatedly reorganized: the number of economic ministers was halved and doubled within a year, and finally cut severely; economic administration was first concentrated, then diffused; the powers of an economic minister were sharply increased, then abolished. Finally, the agency that was supposed to plan the economic activities of these protean bodies was itself subject to remarkable variation in its powers and internal organization. The disruptive effects of these basic administrative changes, and of those later resulting from Khrushchev's penchant for such changes, were substantial. This suggests that the Soviet economy is in a significant degree sensitive to changes in the administrative superstructure, and that the potential political bargaining power of the bureaucratic elite is considerable. It remains a question whether a diffuse and weakened state bureaucracy, even if it is closely directed by a powerful and closely knit Party machine, is adequate to supervise the Soviet economy.

The cleavage between the Party machine and the state bureaucracy, which already existed at Stalin's death, was broadened and deepened by their subsequent conflict. The intensity of this struggle seems incompatible with the West's conception of a Soviet "ruling class" embracing both the Party and the state bureaucracy. Both groups, of course, possess power and privilege far beyond the dreams of mere workers or peasants. But in battling for hegemony, the two antagonists employed potent weapons against each other. The fate of hundreds of economic administrators who were expelled from Moscow testifies to the seriousness of the contest in which they were engaged. Moreover, leaders of the two sides did not scruple in the heat of battle to harm the state, for the high cost in money and confusion did not deter them from repeatedly reorganizing the economic bureaucracy for factional ends. They were even willing to risk grave injury to the Soviet empire in order to gain victory over the domestic enemy, as when Khrushchev delivered the "secret speech" implicating his political opponents in Stalin's crimes.[11] Although the conflict between the Party machine and the state bureaucracy was temporarily resolved without weakening the regime, its severity permits us to speak, in Marxist terms, of an "antagonistic contradiction" between them.

In the past, close control by the Party over state activities was justified on several grounds: the low proportion of Party members to the population (generally less than 2 percent), widespread ideological deviation, growing intensity of class struggle, and prevalence of spying on behalf of foreign powers. But in the 1960s these excuses have lost whatever cogency they once possessed. Virtually all officials in non-Party institutions have for some time

[11] Khrushchev's object in delivering the speech at a secret session of the XX Party Congress was of course not simply to denigrate his opponents. It was also to dispel suspicion that he was an incipient Stalin, to reassure the Party that he would not use terror against it, as Stalin had done, and to destroy Stalin's stifling authority so that he could freely develop his own policies and programs for the USSR. But his hasty pursuit of these objectives undoubtedly injured Soviet interests, particularly in East Europe. See Rush, *The Rise of Khrushchev,* pp. 1, 40–66, 71.

now been Party members; [12] the charge of deviation is now rarely made—almost the worst sin of which officials are now accused is hidebound conservatism; "struggle" between the classes in the USSR has long since been superseded by their "friendship"; and allegedly almost the only spies now to be found in the USSR are recruited from outside the country. Why then is the Party machine's hegemony still required?

In Lenin's day the Party's members, a few hundred thousand all told, controlled the country's political, economic, and cultural institutions, which were largely staffed by non-Communists and anti-Communists. Today, a comparable number of Party *apparatchiks* exercise control over these institutions, even though they are now staffed by many millions of Communists.[13] Need this party within the Party exist and, if so, must it be sovereign? The Party machine has had much to say about its sovereignty since receiving it at Khrushchev's hands in 1957. Yet it remains doubtful that the Party's ten million members, particularly those in key positions of institutions other than the Party machine, have been convinced that state institutions still cannot be trusted to govern the country, and that ultimate power belongs by right and forever to the Party machine. As we shall argue, this may be a critical issue in the Khrushchev succession, as it was after Stalin.

[12] The proportion of the Soviet population that belongs to the Party is now almost 5 percent, around two and one-half times what it was in the 1930s, and more than ten times the average percentage for the first decade of Soviet rule.

[13] The system of surveillance by the Party has changed in important respects since the 1920s but it is no less pervasive than it was then, and no less expressive of distrust towards institutions other than the Party itself.

V: Is There a Khrushchev Succession Problem?

According to our account, Khrushchev resolved the Stalin succession crisis by establishing his personal rule. If he was not supreme, then he was not solely responsible for the comparative stability of Soviet politics after 1957, and there would be slight reason to believe that his political demise would produce a succession crisis. Furthermore, if Khrushchev was not supreme, then he was hardly in a position even to attempt to arrange the succession. It is therefore necessary to consider at some length Khrushchev's place in the leadership during the years when he headed it.

WAS THERE AN OLIGARCHY?

It has sometimes been supposed that Khrushchev was the spokesman for an oligarchy. The chief difficulty with this view is that one cannot readily identify the group of colleagues, or oligarchical body, to whom Khrushchev is supposed to have been responsible. An oligarchical body needs a stable membership; new members must be chosen by co-optation, but at a slow rate so as not to undermine the power of the original members. Actually, the Party

Presidium was such an oligarchy, or "collective leadership," in the years from 1953 to 1957. Of the ten men who made up the Presidium after Stalin's death, the oligarchy purged one, Beria, who was a threat to the other members by reason of his control over the political police, and added two, Suslov and Kirichenko. The oligarchy was fundamentally unstable, however, being a transitional form of rule during the Stalin succession crisis. It was overthrown by Khrushchev in 1957; of its members besides Khrushchev, only Suslov and Mikoyan remained by 1960. For a time Bulganin and Voroshilov were allowed to remain members even though they had been personally discredited within leadership circles. This hardly speaks for the sovereign character of the Presidium.

Even after Khrushchev established his rule, there was a considerable turnover of new Presidium members. His chosen lieutenants were brought into it, but some were later removed when they incurred his displeasure, either by failing to display the requisite zeal and competence or by overreaching the limits of their assigned powers. Thus, Kirichenko and Aristov, who occupied powerful posts at the center of the Party machine, were suddenly deprived of their Party offices in 1960. Ignatov, Belyaev, Furtseva, and Mukhitdinov, after being in the Presidium for four years, were not reelected in 1961.

These six leaders were dropped from the Presidium unobtrusively. On the other hand, the seven members of the "anti-Party group" were subjected to strong personal and political criticism when they were expelled from the Presidium. This contrasting treatment of Khrushchev's critics, who opposed his power, and of his lieutenants, who did not justify his confidence, is instructive, for Stalin, too, maintained such a double standard. In the 1920s, when he purged the Politburo of his enemies, he scathingly attacked their ideological and political failings; but in the 1930s, when he purged the Politburo of lieutenants he had himself raised to that position, he did it silently.[1] As we have already observed, however, the subsequent treatment of purged lieutenants by Stalin, on the one hand, and by Khrushchev, on the other, differed markedly.

As Khrushchev's former favorites were removed, new ones replaced them. After 1960, Podgorny, Polyansky, Voronov, Kirilenko, and Kosygin were added to the Presidium. All but Kosygin were in relatively minor posts when Khrushchev became dictator in 1957, and there is no evidence that any of these five promotions originated otherwise than with him. By mid-1964, the Presidium (in addition to these post-1957 additions, and Khrushchev himself) consisted of a superannuated hack (Shvernik), two leaders elected in 1957 (Kozlov and Brezhnev),[2] and the above-mentioned holdovers, Mikoyan and Suslov. It is difficult to suppose that these men, or some combination among them, controlled the composition of the Presidium during the past half dozen years. They, too, seem to owe their positions and authority to Khrushchev.

Some observers, it is true, suppose that Kozlov or Suslov led factions opposed to Khrushchev. Indeed, before his second illness in 1963, Kozlov's power was substantial, for

[1] A partial exception is the linking of Ya. Rudzutak to the accused in the trial of "Rightists" in 1938.

[2] By 1963 Kozlov was physically incapacitated; Kuusinen, who with Shvernik, Kozlov, and Brezhnev entered the Presidium in 1957 and remained there at Khrushchev's sufferance, died in May, 1964.

he was Khrushchev's deputy in charge of an important part of the Party machine. But that he owed his power to Khrushchev is indicated by the fact that Kozlov was only a provincial Third Secretary when Khrushchev began his rise in 1953.[3] Moreover, his capacity to exercise patronage was limited until May, 1960, when he finally reached the center of power, the Secretariat of the Central Committee. Suslov, although a long-term member of the Secretariat (since 1947), had few opportunities to appoint his partisans to posts in the Party machine. There is evidence that both Kozlov and Suslov[4] at times opposed Khrushchev on particular questions, but there is no reason to believe that they organized a faction to oppose his authority or his policies openly within the Presidium.

While an oligarchy requires stability in the ruling body, the composition of the Presidium, as we have just seen, was markedly unstable. The same is true of the Secretariat of the Central Committee, which is formally subordinate to the Presidium. According to the Party statute (article 39), the Presidium is charged simply with directing the work of the Central Committee between plenums; the Secretariat, with directing current work, mainly in selecting cadres and organizing the verification of fulfillment. In another of its provisions, the statute seems to characterize the Presidium, but not the Secretariat, as a policy-making body like the Central Committee. It requires "systematic turnover of the membership of Party bodies"

[3] In 1952 Kozlov was not elected to the enlarged Presidium which had thirty-six members and candidates.

[4] In two speeches in the spring of 1958 Suslov omitted Khrushchev's name at a time when other Presidium-level speakers made a point of mentioning him.

(article 25), and specifically provides for this with respect to the Central Committee and the Presidium, but not the Secretariat.[5]

Of course, statutory definitions of authority can be deceptive. A weightier argument against the sovereignty of the Secretariat in recent years is that it lost some of its former powers to the Bureau of the Central Committee for the RSFSR (Russian Republic). This Bureau, having been created in 1956 simply by decree of the Central Committee, was authorized to set up a number of "departments" for the Russian Republic corresponding to those previously existing in the Secretariat with jurisdiction throughout the USSR. Subsequently the XXII Party Congress added to the Bureau's permanence and prestige by making it a statutory body (article 39). The original 1956 decree establishing the Bureau made the First Secretary (i.e., Khrushchev) *ex officio* Chairman of the Bureau; [6] in May, 1960, all other Bureau members were removed from the Secretariat. Thereafter, only Khrushchev sat on both the Bureau and the Secretariat, as their head. While members of the Secretariat, other than Khrushchev, were not on the Bureau, Presidium members were, which suggests that the division between the Bureau and the Presidium was less complete, and less significant politically, than the division between the Bureau and the Secretariat.

Whatever its powers, the Secretariat has lacked the stability of an oligarchical body. The eight-man Secretariat elected in June, 1957, had grown to ten members by the

[5] See footnote 10. One-fourth of the Central Committee must be newly elected, although there is no limit on the tenure of individual members.

[6] *Spravochnik Partiinogo Rabotnika* (Handbook for Party Workers) (Moscow, Gospolitizdat, 1957), p. 127.

end of 1959. By mid-1964 only three of the ten were still members of the thirteen-man Secretariat: Khrushchev, Suslov, and Brezhnev, who had been removed from the Secretariat in May, 1960, but subsequently restored to it after a three years' absence.

What of the Central Committee itself? Is it not possible that this body of several hundred men has been the real ruler of Russia in recent years, the oligarchy on which the Presidium, the Secretariat, the Russian Bureau, and even the First Secretary have depended for their power? It is hard to believe this in view of Khrushchev's dictatorial demeanor at its meetings.[7] In any case, the Central Committee, which is charged with directing all work of the Party between Congresses, has been as much in flux as the executive bodies that it formally elects. Around half of the members and candidates elected following the XX Party Congress (1956) were newcomers, as were roughly half of the next Central Committee elected in 1961. Moreover, the present Central Committee's capacity to deliberate was reduced by making it 30 percent larger than its predecessor (330 as compared with 255).

Finally, then, is it possible that the Congress of the CPSU, which chose new Central Committees in 1952, 1956, and 1961, is the sovereign body that we have been searching for? There is a decisive objection to this hypothesis. The Party statute formally grants the Central Committee the power to establish norms of representation for the Congress. In accordance with the norms applied in 1956, fewer than 1,400 voting delegates were chosen; the

[7] See, for example, the stenographic report of the January, 1961, plenum.

norms used in 1961 produced three times as many. Clearly, a political body which is entitled to meet only once every four years and whose size is very elastic could hardly be the sovereign body in the Soviet system.

We are forced to conclude that none of these bodies constituted an oligarchy to which Khrushchev was subject. They evidently were all subject to Khrushchev, being constituted according to his will.[8] This is why Khrushchev's closest lieutenants, when they finally moved to bring him under control, had no recourse but to organize a coup d'état.

In order to control the regime's top bodies, Khrushchev practiced rotation of members. The new Party statute adopted at the XXII Congress in 1961 not only legitimized large turnovers in the Party's bodies, but went so far as to make them mandatory. Even so, only one-fourth of the membership of the top bodies is required to be replaced at each new election, rather than almost one-half as happened the last two times. According to Frol Kozlov, these provisions were included to ensure that the collective did not lose control over individual members.[9] Their effect, however, was to make members of the *apparat* even less secure than formerly. Now they must earn the privilege of remaining in their posts, rather than, as before, having only to avoid the adverse criticism that would bring their removal. Moreover, since exceptionally authoritative leaders are exempted from the provisions which limit members of Party committees to three terms, it appears that control

[8] There were important limits on Khrushchev's power, however, as we shall see.

[9] "CPSU—Party of the Entire People," *World Marxist Review* (June, 1962), p. 7.

by a supreme ruler, rather than by "the collective," was strengthened.[10]

Khrushchev's system of rotation was not inflicted only on members of higher Party bodies, but on lower echelon chiefs as well. By 1962, only one-eighth of provincial (oblast and krai) First Secretaries had held office since 1957, and less than one-third since 1959. Kozlov, who gives these figures, introduces them with the remark: "Those who are unable to keep in step with the times and who persist in the old habits will have to give way to capable, forward-looking people." [11] While many of the former provincial First Secretaries were promoted, transferred, or retired (as incompetent or superannuated), it seems likely that an appreciable number were removed for having at some time opposed Khrushchev or his faction. In any case, the great majority of the provincial First Secretaries under Khrushchev had received their posts during his rule, and were doubtless aware of whose power had removed their predecessors and had installed them.[12]

While Khrushchev ruled, it was often supposed that his only loyal followers were those who, like Brezhnev and Podgorny, had served with him before the Stalin succession. Had he really acted on this assumption, Khrushchev would have placed unnecessary and almost impossible restrictions upon himself in staffing the agencies of his rule.

[10] The sole exception to this provision is the Central Committee of the CPSU, whose members are not limited to three terms. Since the tenure of Secretaries of the Central Committee is not specifically limited either, there is no special obstacle to their serving indefinitely.

[11] "CPSU—Party of the Entire People," *World Marxist Review* (June, 1962), p. 7.

[12] "The principal posts in the Party are filled by people who have come to the fore thanks to a profound knowledge of life and *ability correctly to implement the policies of the Party.*" *Ibid.*, emphasis added.

Before he began his rise to power, his career, unlike Stalin's, was for the most part limited to work in provincial Party organizations: in Moscow from 1932 to 1938; in the Ukraine from 1938 to 1949; and in Moscow once more from 1949 to 1953, although by this time he had also entered the central Secretariat. There was no reason, however, why Khrushchev should have drawn his subordinates only from the quite limited group of men he had encountered in these organizations at these times. Once he became head of the Secretariat in 1953, he secured control over a most powerful institution, and was doubtless able to win over many of its members. He won numerous additional adherents after he defeated his rivals in the Presidium and gained control over the entire regime. The loyalty of his subordinates was to depend not on the length of their association with him, nor even on gratitude for the benefits he had conferred upon them, but rather on their estimate of his power to bestow future benefits and to punish acts of disloyalty.

THE RULE OF KHRUSHCHEV

Quite apart from the difficulty in identifying an organ or faction that opposed Khrushchev's authority, there is much positive evidence of his sovereign power. Khrushchev completely dominated the two Party Congresses that were held after he achieved supremacy in 1957, especially the XXII Congress: its first two days were almost entirely devoted to his addresses, and not until the third day did another major leader get to speak. Stenographic reports of the Central Committee plenums show him dominating their proceedings as well. He stood in judgment on the speakers, even criticizing members of the Presidium, interrupted at will, castigated those who displeased him (and subsequently saw to it, at least in some instances, that they were duly punished), and generally acted the despot. It appears from the published reports that the speakers, especially those criticized by Khrushchev, treated him with a deference bordering on subservience.

After 1957, Khrushchev became the source of doctrinal change and controversy in the world Communist movement, modifying the official ideology, if not systematically, at least in accordance with the needs of practice. He brought about large reforms of the Soviet system and enacted the Party's new program, the first in over forty years, which formally established the pattern and direction of Soviet development for the next two decades, and was offered as a model for any nation that wished to become Communist. He engaged extensively in personal diplomacy, with the heads of Western governments as well as with those of emergent nations of Asia and Africa. He spoke for the USSR both at the United Nations and at assemblies of the world Communist movement. His lieutenants have credited him with the initiative in establishing policies in their own spheres of activity and in the various divisions of statecraft: foreign policy, agriculture, housing, industrial administration, and Party affairs. In the sphere of military strategy, where there were revolutionary developments both in Soviet weaponry and doctrine, Khrushchev had the key role. His speech in January, 1960, was the most comprehensive and authoritative statement on defense policy in many years, although that policy was modified, in part, in its implementation. It was on his initiative, according to Defense Minister Malinovsky's speech at the XXII Party Congress, that strategic rocket troops were established. At times, it is true, Khrushchev's role in defense policy was deprecated: there are intimations of this in *Voennaia Strategiia* (Military Strategy), edited by Marshal Sokolovskii in 1962. Subsequently, however, important military writers took pains to eulogize Khrushchev's personal role in the formulation of Soviet military strategy and doctrine, including its more technical aspects.[13]

The cult of Khrushchev was established and, despite some setbacks, made good progress. His preeminence came to be acknowledged in ritualistic formulas, such as "the Central Committee, headed by N. S. Khrushchev." Whole books were published exhibiting Khrushchev the miner or Khrushchev the corn expert. His military contributions to the winning of the Great Fatherland War were duly recorded in accounts of the partisan movement and of battles at Volgograd (once Stalingrad) and elsewhere. In honorary nominations preceding elections to the Supreme Soviet in 1962, Khrushchev's total was well over twice that of the men who came next, Brezhnev and Kozlov.

In speeches and articles after 1957, all major leaders performed the rites of the Khrushchev cult, if with varying degrees of fervor. They made a point of mentioning his name, though they infrequently mentioned each other's and he rarely mentioned theirs. They praised Khrushchev's fight for peace, knowledge of affairs, closeness to the people, loyalty to Lenin, and theoretical prowess; but if any of them possess special political qualities, there was little

[13] See, for example, Marshal Malinovsky's pamphlet, *Bditel'no stoiat' na strazhe mira* (Vigilantly Stand Guard Over the Peace) (Moscow, Voenizdat, 1962), pp. 9, 22–23, 43–44.

to display them. Compared to Khrushchev, they small and obscure, just as Khrushchev did in day.

So far as formal authority is concerned, by 1958 Khrushchev sat on all the chief organs of dictatorship: 1) the Presidium, 2) the Secretariat, 3) the Bureau for the Russian Republic of the Central Committee, and 4) the Council of Ministers; after 1960, no other leader was on more than two of these bodies. Khrushchev held the leading posts in the Party, the government, and the army, being First Secretary of the Central Committee, Chairman of the Council of Ministers, and Supreme Commander-in-Chief of the Armed Forces, a post Stalin did not formally assume until war time.

LIMITS ON KHRUSHCHEV'S RULE

While Khrushchev controlled the levers of power and possessed supreme authority like Stalin in the early 1930s, he was never the autocrat the world came to know in the person of Stalin. A consequence of Khrushchev's exercise of personal dictatorship through a single sovereign agency of rule was that his political will met resistance and was not fully realized. He himself alluded to views opposed to his own on particular questions involving Party organization, military affairs, education, and diplomacy. In the area of economic policy, there was considerable discussion and public controversy, especially on questions involving the allocation of resources to major sectors of the economy: consumer goods industry, agriculture, defense, and heavy industry. It is clear that Khrushchev's word was not simply law, for more than once after he had said his word the law turned out otherwise. Such things as these led some Western observers to assume that Khrushchev was the creature of sovereign bodies or groups in the USSR, even though they could not identify them. Khrushchev was allowed to speak for these groups, it was supposed, but they were able to decide for themselves. Since Khrushchev controlled the key political bodies, however, it seems more likely that he allowed collective discussion, in which specialists also participated, but finally decided himself in the light of authoritative opinion and the circumstances prevailing at the time the decision was made.[14] Khrushchev unquestionably was constrained by proximate political pressures, but there is little evidence that they compelled him to act contrary to his judgment.

Khrushchev's political lieutenants wrote articles and published speeches, but these contained little that was original. For the most part they repeated and illustrated what Khrushchev had already said or dealt concretely with assigned areas of responsibility; certainly there is little evidence of consistent opposition by any of them to Khrushchev's major policies. It is the prerogative of the ruler to consult with experts, and Khrushchev accorded them a much greater voice in the formative stage of policy deliberations than they ever had been given previously. But Khrushchev did not hesitate to attack them, and even on occasion to deprive them of their positions, when they were too critical of his pet proposals.

Perhaps the most striking evidence of Khrushchev's per-

[14] For example, the one-third cut in military personnel which he had adopted in January, 1960, was certainly opposed by important elements in the military establishment; yet it was not until the United States sent military units to Europe, in connection with the Berlin crisis, in mid-1961, that Khrushchev publicly rescinded that decision.

sonal rule and of the stability it gave to Soviet politics was his capacity to maintain his power despite the failure of his policies. His agricultural program, to which he committed much of his personal prestige, largely foundered from 1959 to 1963. Under him, the USSR lost its leading position not only in the Communist world as a whole, but even in parts of East Europe. Communist China (the CPR) was transformed from an ally into an intransigent foe, and though Khrushchev was by no means wholly responsible for this development, his attempts to exert pressure on the CPR were so crude and inept as to cause a rapid widening of the breach between the two sides. Khrushchev's campaign against West Berlin from 1958 to 1962 not only failed to undermine the Western position in Berlin, but contributed to a rise of almost one-half in U.S. military spending that left the USSR far behind the United States in intercontinental striking power.[15] Khrushchev's subsequent effort to rectify the military balance led to the humiliating withdrawal of Soviet missiles from Cuba in 1962. The immediate effects of these and other major defeats, which were not offset by victories of comparable magnitude, were surprisingly slight. Khrushchev's leadership appeared unshaken by this series of shocks and his power was not visibly diminished. In view of the sharp setbacks

[15] As a result of these increased expenditures, which were partly stimulated by Khrushchev's actions, U.S. military might in mid-1964 was described by President Johnson in these words: "In the past three years, we have increased our nuclear power on alert two and one-half times. . . . We have now more than 1,000 fully armed ICBM and Polaris missiles ready for retaliation. The Soviet Union has far fewer, and none ready to be launched beneath the seas. We have more than 1,100 strategic bombers. . . . The Soviet Union, we estimate, could, with difficulty, send less than one-third of this number over targets in the United States." Speech to the Coast Guard Academy, June 3, printed in the New York *Times,* June 4, 1964.

to Soviet policy, the wonder is the stability of Soviet politics while Khrushchev ruled, not the perturbations that occurred, which doubtless would have been far greater in a period of succession like that which followed Stalin's death.

Actually, the perturbations in Soviet policy arising from opposition to Khrushchev's policies seem no greater than those encountered by Stalin in the early years of his dictatorship (roughly from 1930 to 1936), or for that matter by Lenin. Lenin was strongly opposed on many crucial questions in the regime's early years, sometimes even by a majority, but because he was Lenin he always succeeded in finally having his way. Until he was incapacitated by illness, no major step was taken which did not either originate with him or secure his approval. Stalin, too, in the early years of his dictatorship, was opposed, and even overruled, by the men whom he had brought to power; but he *had* brought them to power, and they *did* recognize his preeminence.[16] Both Lenin and the early Stalin are generally recognized to have been dictators, and unless the word has changed its meaning, it is applicable to Khrushchev's rule as well.

Khrushchev's rule in the period 1957–1964 may be characterized as a *limited dictatorship*. What accounted for the limits on his power? They arose in part from the nature of the Soviet political system. Since there is no formal place in it for a dictator, a dictator must give the appearance of deferring to authoritative bodies in the sphere of his action. Khrushchev, unlike Hitler for example, formally had to justify his policies before the Central Committee

16 See, for example, the articles written for his fiftieth birthday, December 21, 1929.

and the Party Congress. This formal requirement could have important political consequences, as when the arguments he employed were quickly invalidated by new developments. This may have happened, for example, in the leadership's discussions of the U-2 incident of May, 1960, which took place while the Supreme Soviet was in session. It is significant that Stalin, after he had succeeded in terrorizing the Soviet leadership, convened only two Party Congresses (and spoke only briefly to the second, in 1952); he called few meetings of the Central Committee; and had only irregular meetings of the Politburo in his last years. It was as if he had to dispense with such formalities in order to make his autocracy truly effective.

A second major source of limits on Khrushchev's power arose from the character of his political and economic reforms. He tried to provide new incentives for higher productivity throughout the economy, as well as to encourage initiative on the lower echelons. While he failed to provide the stable political and administrative structure that this scheme required, as long as he continued to aim at enlisting the energies and commitment of the administrative and professional classes, he had to take their attitudes and desires into consideration.

Khrushchev's personal dictatorship was limited also by his own history. He lacked the prestige of achievement which made Lenin the universally recognized leader—not by reason of his office or his function, but because he was the founder of both the Party and the state. Khrushchev lacked, moreover, the popular authority that Stalin had won as the architect of victory in Russia's war against the Germans. He could retain what prestige he had only by avoiding additional defeats, and he could gain the prestige of a successful dictator only by winning new victories. In lieu of these, he was compelled to rely on the cult of Khrushchev and on his control of the levers of power.

On the other hand, Khrushchev was unable to suppress dissent in his subordinates by the imminent threat of terrible sanctions. He could reduce their power, or even deprive them of it; but he could not effectively threaten his lieutenants with imprisonment or death. When Stalin, in the mid-1930s, found his lieutenants reluctant to imprison, and especially to execute, his defeated rivals, he subjected them to the great purge; a quarter century later, however, when Soviet society had changed radically, when Khrushchev's associates had been duly warned by History speaking with Khrushchev's own voice, when Khrushchev was well into the seventh decade of his life, so drastic a solution was not available to him.

Khrushchev was finally overthrown by a conspiracy, like other rulers of our day. But while he occupied the supreme offices of the Party and the government, he gave a stability to Soviet politics that it may not know again for some time. Moreover, as supreme ruler, Khrushchev could attempt to arrange an orderly succession. To do so, however, he had to sacrifice some of the power and authority he had arrogated to himself after Stalin's death. Since his was a limited dictatorship, he had to be especially cautious in arranging the succession so as not to endanger his rule. He did what he thought could be done prudently; to his sorrow, he learned that he had done too much.

VI: Khrushchev's Succession Arrangements

While he ruled Russia, Khrushchev was the best witness to his own power. When he gave an order a part of the vast mechanism that was at his command began to move. It may not have moved as he wanted it to, and it may shortly have lost its motion, but for the moment he could observe a response. However aware he may have been of the resistance of this vast machine to his expressed will, and Khrushchev complained repeatedly of this, he could not but be impressed by his part in the working of the system, and doubtless believed that the system required him to go on playing his part. Stalin thought of himself as indispensable—as when he asked his heirs: "If I should die, what will become of you?" [1] Khrushchev, though less susceptible to this conceit, was probably in some measure infected with it.

A dictator, because he believes in his indispensability, must wonder how the system will work without him. There is a tension between the ruler's belief in his indispensability and his concern for the future of the regime

[1] The incident was told by Mikoyan in an election speech on February 26, 1959, as broadcast by the Rostov Oblast Regional Service, February 28, 1959. It was not in the abbreviated version carried by the central press.

after he is gone. Once he is confronted with the problem of succession, a ruler seems bound to make some effort to cope with it, unless, like the classical tyrant, he rules solely to gratify his own desires; but to arrange the succession, as we have argued, strains the powers of the wisest leader. He must make the attempt, yet it will probably fail.

Then are his dispositions for the succession inconsequential and unrewarding for study? Surely not. Lenin's testament, it is true, failed to thwart Stalin's drive to power, yet its role in the denigration of Stalin at the XX Congress was not insignificant; previously, the testament had contributed to the unleashing of the great blood purges of the 1930s. Similarly, though Stalin failed to consummate the doctor-affair, his beginning it was to influence the politics of the Stalin succession for at least the next three years. Moreover, even if the ruler's plans for the succession are not wholly realized, they may still have a partial success. If, as we shall argue, Khrushchev tried to deal with the problem of succession, his dispositions did not lose their significance because he was ousted before he could achieve his purpose. On the contrary, his succession arrangements shaped the situation that resulted from his fall, and even helped to bring it about.

Khrushchev was deeply aware of the Soviet succession problem, although Marxism contributed little to that awareness. Preoccupied with the problem of the transfer of power from one class to another, it has relatively little to say about the transfer of power between rulers. Khrushchev learned of the succession problem through experience—not theory. He was already in his thirties during the Lenin succession, and he in some measure relived that experience in his campaign against Stalin's memory. The

Stalin succession was still more vivid for Khrushchev because he had so recently been the chief protagonist in it.

Khrushchev's concern about his own succession was evident. On a number of occasions he spoke of his advanced age, and even of his coming death, a subject that Bolsheviks ordinarily avoid.[2] According to Soviet laws, "I am already working overtime. . . . But I feel in myself forces, a great surge of energy. Why, shall I take it with me into the grave?! No!"[3] He explicitly called attention to the time when he would not be the country's leader. In the spring of 1963, when he found it necessary to defend the authoritarian principle in the Soviet system against the attacks of intellectuals, Khrushchev said he did this out of regard for the Party, the people, Communism, but not out of regard for "some special position of my own in the party. . . . I am already sixty-nine years old. . . . Surely everyone understands that the post I now occupy in the Party and the state I cannot occupy forever."[4] As early as 1959, he spoke to Averell Harriman of his intention of avoiding Stalin's mistake in failing to designate a successor.[5]

[2] See N. Leites, *A Study of Bolshevism,* (Glencoe, Ill., Free Press, 1953), Chapter III.

[3] Speech to the XIV Komsomol Congress, April 19, 1962, printed in *Pravda,* April 21, 1962. Significantly, Khrushchev could not refer to his death without speaking of his present vitality, which illustrates the tension between the belief in his indispensability and his concern for the future of the regime. See also his concluding remarks to the Party Congress: "Time will pass, we shall die, we are all mortal, but as long as we continue to work we can and must find out many things and tell the truth to the Party and the people." *XXII S"ezd KPSS* (The XXII Congress of the CPSU) (Moscow, Gospolitizdat, 1962), II, 584.

[4] *Pravda,* April 26, 1963.

[5] Averell Harriman, *Peace With Russia?* (New York, Simon and Schuster, 1959), p. 105. While Stalin may not have appointed a successor formally (or he may have—Khrushchev was not a disinterested party in the matter), I believe he made it clear that Malenkov was to be his chief heir.

The problem of arranging his succession could not be solved simply by securing the succession for a designated heir, however, contrary to what Khrushchev implied in his conversation with Harriman. Moreover, while Nicholas II set himself the goal of passing on to his successor the whole of the inheritance that he had received from his predecessor, this was hardly Khrushchev's object. For him, choosing the successor was a means to larger ends.

Khrushchev could reasonably expect his place in the Communist movement to become a central issue in any struggle over his succession, just as Stalin's person and policies became a central issue after he died. He knew that his program for the realization of Communism, which the XXII Party Congress had adopted, would be at stake as well as his whole conception of the kind of society that was to be created out of the human and social materials that had been formed by Stalin's titanic will. Khrushchev's vindication in the quarrel with Mao, as well as Soviet hegemony in the world Communist movement, depended in part on his skill in arranging the succession. Moreover, Soviet historiography being what it is, the account of Khrushchev's reign in future Party histories clearly depended in large measure on the course and outcome of the succession crisis brought on by his downfall.

To pursue his various and partially conflicting objectives reasonably, Khrushchev had to order them according to some scheme of priorities. No doubt he would have liked to solve the problem of succession in the USSR once and for all, but this objective did not dominate his succession arrangements. On the other hand, Khrushchev set high store on assuring his good name in Soviet history and wanted an heir who would realize his version of what Soviet society should be. He meant the Party apparatus to retain its hegemony; yet he might conceivably have risked even this in order to prevent ill-qualified blowhards from again acquiring a dominant position in it. He wanted to order the succession so that the Soviet Union would not be weakened during the transition, but this was not an absolute and overriding objective. Just as Khrushchev waged the struggle for the Stalin succession ruthlessly, and willingly risked weakening the USSR, as when he delivered the secret speech, so he might have preferred a temporary weakening of the USSR to the abandonment of his basic policies.

Succession, as it presented itself to Khrushchev, had two parts: the institutional problem and the personality problem. A discussion of his strategy for coping with each follows.

THE INSTITUTIONAL PROBLEM

An orderly succession requires that the institutions of dictatorship be so arranged that they will not be in conflict during the period of succession. If the inherited system of rule cannot operate effectively at that time, then the succession crisis will transcend personalities and factions and bring about a struggle for power involving the major institutions. Stalin's system of rule had become so highly personal that it was not viable without him. On the other hand, Khrushchev's system of rule, while it reflected his powerful personality, was not unique: in its essentials it resembled the system of rule employed by Stalin in the first years of his dictatorship. Now, if such diverse personalities as Khrushchev and Stalin managed with such a system, presumably some future dictator, if properly qualified, could do as well. Moreover, this mode of rule has demonstrated its flexibility, for it proved an effective instrument for carrying out both social revolution under Stalin, and social reform under Khrushchev. For Khrushchev, the solution to the institutional problem, apparently, was to assure that his system of rule remained intact during the period of succession. The kingpin in that system, as noted above, was the hegemony of the Party machine.

Khrushchev's rise to power during the Stalin succession was based on the Party machine. It was not a tool only in the succession struggle, however, but was Khrushchev's chosen instrument of dictatorial rule and policy-making. Despite his repeated administrative reorganizations and his experimentation with various devices for managing Soviet society, the Party machine not only remained sovereign, but strengthened its grip on the other agencies of rule. Administrators and technicians were brought into the Party apparatus in good numbers to improve its capacity to control the economic bureaucracy from top to bottom. A late trend toward recentralization somewhat strengthened governmental economic bodies, but the capacity of the central Party apparatus to intervene in the economy increased even more. After 1958 the political police was headed by Party *apparatchiks* instead of, as before, by men who had made careers in the state security ranks. The Party's control over the armed forces was intensified and the number of controlling agencies increased to provide a highly intricate system under the close direction of the Party Secretariat.

In the attempt to assure Party hegemony after his leaving, Khrushchev made it a principle of Communist theory.

He not only elevated the Party, but, at the same time, deprived the state of much of the prestige and authority that Stalin had conferred on it, especially during the last period of his rule when the state became virtually coordinate with the Party. Initially, Khrushchev's depreciation of the state may have been designed chiefly to consolidate his victory over the state bureaucracy. But his subsequent declaration that the withering of the Soviet state had begun, and his elaboration of the doctrine that "public organizations" would replace state organs as Soviet society moved toward Communism, suggest that he had larger ends in view.

The doctrine of the state's withering away after the proletariat's seizure of power is highly charged with emotion for Marxists. Before the Bolshevik Revolution, both Engels and Lenin stated that the state would begin to wither as soon as the proletariat seized power. After the Revolution, however, Stalin denied that the Soviet state was withering, and suggested that the state would not even begin to wither until a "socialist encirclement" had replaced capitalist encirclement.[6] Khrushchev reversed Stalin's dictum in a major speech shortly after establishing his personal rule in late 1957: "The Marxist-Leninist teaching on the state, on its withering in the degree (*po mere*) that society moves towards complete Communism, has tremendous importance." [7] A week later, when asked by Henry Shapiro about the theory of the gradual wither-

[6] "Report on the Work of the Central Committee to the XVIII Congress of the CPSU (B)," March 10, 1939, I. Stalin, *Voprosy leninizma* (Problems of Leninism) (Moscow, Gospolitizdat, 1947), pp. 602–603, 606. See also "Kommunizm," *Politicheskii Slovar* (Political Dictionary) (Moscow, Gospolitizdat, 1940), p. 270.

[7] *Pravda,* November 7, 1957.

ing of the state, Khrushchev replied: "Strictly speaking this process is already going on."

The seriousness of Khrushchev's purpose in asserting that the Soviet state was withering is suggested by the persistence with which he sought to overcome the firm opposition that it encountered. The thesis was usually skirted in subsequent discussions of the state's role in the transition to Communism. Although it was included in the Party's important textbook, *Fundamentals of Marxism-Leninism,* the authors' manner revealed the controversy surrounding the thesis, and perhaps their own reservations:

Thus one may say that the withering of the state is in fact already going on. . . . In view of this [certain "complications"] *can we speak of* the withering of the state? *Yes we can* because the general trend of development in the period of transition to Communism is in this direction.[8]

Despite the reserve with which it was received, Khrushchev made it clear that he intended his thesis to be incorporated in the Party program:

Allow me to mention a number of theoretical problems dealt with by our Party in recent years. . . . In our country where there have long been no exploiting classes, the gradual withering of the organs of state administrative government is going on. . . . These and other questions concerning the theory and practice of building Communism will be reflected in the new program of the CPSU.[9]

[8] Emphasis added. *Osnovi Marksizma-Leninizma* (Fundamentals of Marxism-Leninism) (Moscow, Gospolitizdat, 1959), pp. 721–22.

[9] *Pravda,* January 25, 1961. Controversy regarding the withering of the state continued in the following months while the Party program was being drafted. That controversy was frankly discussed by the prominent jurist, P. Romashkin: "From this it is clear that the withering of the state is already going on. Yet some authors depict the matter as though, until the complete construction of Communism, there will occur only the process of creating the conditions for the withering of the state, but the

Nevertheless, the program, when it was published, did not contain the thesis that the Soviet state is withering. The reason, presumably, was that Khrushchev had come to believe that the doctrine went too far in depreciating the state.[10] The thesis has its drawbacks. Since the Party continued to rely heavily on the coercive functions of the state, belief in its withering could have unsettling implications that might not be adequately neutralized by the complementary thesis of the growing role of the Party. Hence Khrushchev's caution: the state has begun to wither, yet it is not being weakened; it is losing some of its functions to public organizations, and will lose more of them, yet the state's role in the building of Communism is undiminished. The dialectical character of the withering process had a quality suspiciously like self-contradiction, but Khrushchev's purpose, at any rate, was clear: to legislate the permanent inferiority of the state to the Party, hence of the state bureaucracy to the Party machine.

As noted above, a fundamental source of instability in Soviet succession crises is the chronic conflict among the

---

withering itself will begin only under complete Communism. [This was essentially Stalin's position.] It seems to me that such arguments are based on a misunderstanding. Comrade N. S. Khrushchev directly declared that the withering of the state is already going on in our country. . . . It is necessary, consequently, to proceed on this basis *(iskhodit iz togo, chto)* that the withering of the state is not only something that will take place somehow and in a certain more or less distant future, but something that is happening in the life of our generation." *Partiinaia Zhizn'*, No. 9 (1961), pp. 10–11.

10 The arguments of opponents of the thesis may have had some effect (perhaps including those of the Chinese Communist leaders—see the letter of the CCP Central Committee, June 14, 1963), yet the decision evidently was Khrushchev's own. Oddly, the only speaker at the XXII Congress (which adopted the Party program) who voiced the thesis on the withering of the state was M. A. Suslov, who is widely reputed to be the arch-Stalinist. *Pravda*, October 23, 1961.

instruments of dictatorship, chiefly between the Party machine and the state bureaucracy. Their use as bases of power in the struggle for the succession to Stalin hurt the regime politically and economically, and might have had far more serious consequences had Khrushchev not succeeded in 1957 in leading the Party machine to a decisive victory over the state bureaucracy. Khrushchev's thesis on the state's withering was probably designed, in part, to impair the ability of the state bureaucracy to contest the Party's hegemony in any future crisis.[11]

A natural complement of the classical doctrine of the withering of the state would seem to be a doctrine of the withering of the Party. This association of doctrines has in fact been asserted both practically and theoretically in Yugoslavia, where the transformation of the Communist Party into the Communist League has accompanied the "withering" of the state. In Khrushchev's scheme, however, the complement to the doctrine of the "withering" of the state was the thesis of the increasing political and organizational role of the Party in the transition to Communism. Having relied principally on the Party machine in both his rise to dictatorship and his exercise of it, Khrushchev undertook to assure its hegemony in the future.

"The period of full-scale building of Communism," the program says, "*is characterized* by further growth of the role and importance of the Communist Party as the lead-

[11] The thesis obviously was meant to serve other important ends as well. It underlined the claim that the USSR relies less on coercion than it formerly did, and gave substance to the contention that the USSR is building Communism. Moreover, the doctrine of the withering of the state was basically congenial to Khrushchev. Of the three chief agencies of social control in the USSR—the state bureaucracy, the Party machine, and public opinion—he strongly preferred to rely on the Party machine and public opinion.

ing and directing force of Soviet society." [12] By making the Party's increasing role "characterize" the transition to Communism, the program took an intermediate position between that of the XXI Congress, which said "experience" shows this,[13] and the position of *Kommunist* and other journals, which called the Party's increasing role "an objectively determined process . . . a law (*zakonomernost*)." [14]

The variations on this key formula are certainly notable. Yet granting that the Party's increasing role is not a "law" but merely "characterizes" the transition to Communism, *this new doctrine makes it more dangerous to advocate the government's primacy over the Party machine.* Any leader who does so while the program stands will reveal himself an opponent of Communism. Once again, the tendency of this new thesis, like that of the withering of the state, is to impair the political potential of the state bureaucracy

[12] Emphasis added. See also *Osnovi Marksizma-Leninizma,* p. 723.

[13] "The whole experience of the struggle for the victory of Socialism and Communism shows that in the process of building Communist society the role of the Party, as the experienced vanguard of the people and the highest form of public organization, increasingly grows." Resolution on Khrushchev's Report.

An authoritative writer on Party affairs, G. Shitarev, quoted this passage and boldly undertook to amplify it. "This brief and laconic formula expresses what is most important and essential, what characterizes the process of the further development of the Party itself—the raising of its role, and consequently also the intensification of its political, intellectual (*ideinogo*) and organizational influence on all sides of the life of society to the extent that it advances to the higher phase of Communism. The content of the process, that is, the growing role of the Party, bares an objective character, is determined by the very conditions of the building of Communism." "The Party and the Building of Communism," *Politicheskoe Samoobrazovanie,* No. 8 (1960).

[14] "The Growing Role of the Party in the Building of Communism," *Kommunist,* No. 7 (1959). This was a highly authoritative article: it replaced the customary editorial, and the names of its authors—two of them editors of *Kommunist*—were given only at the end of the article.

in any future succession crisis. Taken together, the two theses seem designed to assure the Party machine's victory in any future succession crisis, if possible by deterring any effort to employ the state bureaucracy as a base for struggle. Of course, it may be argued that words alone are not a sufficient means for assuring the realization of the ruler's will after he has lost or given up his power. Certainly the many millions of words in praise of Stalin that were written or uttered in his lifetime did not prevent his condemnation when he was dead. But in his efforts to influence the events that will follow his death, the ruler is ultimately compelled to rely on words, and their incorporation in the Party program can give them a gravity they would not otherwise possess.

A final and crucial source of limitation on Khrushchev's power, as suggested earlier, was his attempt to base his rule on a single sovereign institution, the Party machine. This deprived him of the pervasive personal control that could be obtained through a system of mutual surveillance by competing institutions. He had to rely in substantial measure on the competence and loyalty of his subordinates in the sovereign Party machine, and on the use of argument to gain their support of particular measures. Stalin, when he ruled by similar means during the first years of his supremacy, met with occasional defiance or covert opposition from his chief lieutenants and provincial satraps, and on the lower levels his commands did not always meet with a full response. To overcome these disadvantages of rule based on a sovereign institution, Stalin deprived the Party machine of its sovereignty, and established instead an intricate system of institutional balances and checks in which terror had a key role, and of which he was the autocratic master. This he accomplished during the great purge of 1936–1938. The principal object of the purge was not to give the Soviet regime totalitarian control over society, which it had already acquired by means of Stalin's "revolution from above"; it was rather to give Stalin autocratic power in the Soviet regime. Its result was to keep Stalin's will from being seriously challenged in the remaining decade and a half of his reign.

In the effort to make his power secure, Khrushchev had to rely upon far less violent means. He divided the Party machine into distinct parts, which were united only in his own person. The two chief divisions were the Secretariat, which deals with the republics of the minority nationalities but whose authority in the Russian Republic is limited, and the Bureau for the Russian Republic; after 1960, only Khrushchev was a member of both bodies. The central apparatus was further divided into territorial and economic bureaus, between which there was almost certainly controversy that could be finally resolved only by the Secretariat or Presidium, or by Khrushchev personally. Similarly there were separate bureaus for industry and agriculture in the Central Committee of the CPSU, as well as in those of the republics, that had to compete for priority in the use of the very limited resources that were available. At the middle levels (oblast and krai) the Party organizations were virtually bifurcated into industrial and agricultural branches. The policing of the economy was entrusted to a separate body, the Party-dominated Committee for Party and State Control; the policing of culture to still another body, the Ideological Commission. These measures reinforced the previously existing tendency of Party cadres to become specialists, like their opposite numbers in economic institutions. In addition to these numerous divisions in the Party machine, Khrushchev tried to balance politically the central as against the provincial apparatus. For a time he counterpoised the two most powerful provincial organizations, the Leningrad and the Ukrainian; subsequently, in the last year of his rule, he balanced two groupings of former members of the Ukrainian Party organization.

Khrushchev relied on these and similar prophylactic devices to secure his power against political challenges, since he could not employ terror to cow his subordinates as Stalin did. By such means he largely succeeded in imposing his basic policies on the men he had raised to positions of leadership, but these proved inadequate to prevent a conspiracy against him. Not surprisingly, once he was overthrown his heirs began to unify what he had divided.

OLIGARCHY OR PERSONAL RULE?

From Lenin's "testament" and other writings of his last period it appears that he meant an oligarchy to succeed him. It was to consist of an enlarged Central Committee, dominated by no one man, but led, perhaps, by an inner group of his closest associates. Stalin's conception of the mode of rule appropriate for his successor is less clear. He expressed doubts openly to his subordinates as to whether any, or all of them together, were capable of ruling the Soviet Union without him. Since these men had all been raised to power by Stalin, his opinion was not lightly dismissed: "We thought of this and wondered how we would manage." [15] In so far as Stalin had a definite conception of the mode of rule that he wanted to come after his own, it

[15] Mikoyan, election speech on February 26, 1959.

may have been of a weakened form of personal dictatorship, one appropriate to the diminished talents of his heir.

For Lenin, the prerogatives of dictatorial rule derived from his possession of the transcendant political wisdom that enabled him to create the Communist Party and establish the Soviet state. He could indicate that an oligarchy should succeed him since he saw no need for an individual to inherit such powers. Khrushchev, on the other hand, seemed to view his supreme position almost as an office that the Party requires, and for the exercise of which the incumbent receives the mandate of the whole Party. He spoke of himself (in the third person) as having been "promoted to the post of First Secretary of the Central Committee by the will of the Party." [16]

An alternative method of rule by a small core of leaders in the Presidium, perhaps the only viable alternative to personal rule, was apparently rejected by him. He maintained that "collective leadership" (the Soviet euphemism for nonpersonal, or oligarchical, rule) inheres in the unwieldy, 330-man, Central Committee (and in the various provincial Party committees), not in the Presidium. The American journalist Henry Shapiro asked: "When you speak about collective leadership [actually, Khrushchev did so infrequently], do you have in mind the Central Committee or the Presidium of the C.C.?" Khrushchev replied: "The Central Committee is meant. The Presidium is the executive organ of the Central Committee." [17] Khru-

[16] Concluding speech to the XXII Congress. See *XXII S"ezd KPSS,* II, 592. See also *Pravda,* September 20, 1964, p. 2, where he says "the people and the Party" made him First Secretary.

[17] *Pravda,* November 19, 1957, p. 2. On the other hand, M. Saburov, seeking to show his support for Khrushchev at the famous meeting of the Presidum in June, 1957, says he then "declared that collective leadership

shchev's view on the restricted competence of the Presidium contrasts with that of Lenin, who spoke of "collegial decisions of the Central Committee *adopted in the Orgburo or Politburo,* or in the plenum of the Central Committee." [18] It is noteworthy that Khrushchev spoke better of the Presidium, perhaps under compulsion, in the period before he succeeded in consolidating his personal rule.[19] But in late 1962 he even began to publish his memoranda addressed to the Presidium, thus depriving it of some of the privacy of its deliberations. This practice continued until his ouster in 1964.

Khrushchev's view that collective leadership inheres in the Central Committee rather than in the Presidium is reflected in a provision of the Party statute first adopted in 1961. Presidium members are not to be elected for more than three successive terms, and the same is true of provincial Party committees; but Central Committee members are not thus restricted, presumably because they formally constitute the Party's collective leadership and are meant to provide continuity of rule. Moreover, at least one-fourth of the Presidium membership is to be newly elected every four years.[20] Thus, rotation of the Presid-

is being realized in the Presidium of the Central Committee." *Vneocherednoi XXI S"ezd KPSS* (Extraordinary XXI Congress of the CPSU) (Moscow, Gospolitizdat, 1959), II, 291.

18 Emphasis added. Speech to IX Party Congress, quoted by L. Slepov and G. Shitarev, "Leninist Norms of Party Life and the Principles of Party Leadership," in *Kommunist,* No. 6 (April, 1955), p. 66.

19 See, for example, his report of the Central Committee to the XX Party Congress. "The Presidium of the C.C. has become a regularly functioning collective organ which has within its field of vision all the more important questions of the life of Party and country." *XX S"ezd Kommunisticheskoi Partii Sovetskogo Soiuza* (The Twentieth Congress of the CPSU) (Moscow, Gospolitizdat, 1956), I, 101.

20 This provision (which also affects the Central Committee) was first applied in 1961. The limit of three terms for Presidium members, however, presumably will have no effect until 1969, or possibly 1973.

ium, which Khrushchev practiced after 1957 as a means of securing his personal rule, was legislated for the period of succession (and beyond) as well. Moreover, certain Presidium members are exempted from this provision, in a passage which is probably as close as the Party statutes of the CPSU have ever come to authorizing the rule of a personal leader:

> Presidium members shall as a rule be elected for not more than three successive terms. Particular Party workers may, by virtue of their recognized authority and high political, organizational, or other abilities, be successively elected to executive bodies for a longer period. In such cases, election requires a majority of at least three-fourths of the votes cast by closed [secret] ballot.

The significance of this new rule proscribing stability in the Presidium's membership is apparent when we recall developments in the Lenin and Stalin successions. In both cases, the Presidium (or Politburo, the analogous body) had a certain stability. For a time, its members were accorded immunity from removal, whether by mutual agreement of that body or by reason of some wider consensus.[21] They could be subjected to strong criticism by the Party's highest bodies, as Trotsky and Malenkov were, and still remain in the Presidium to harass a would-be dictator.

This need not be true, however, in the Khrushchev succession. Since the removal of at least one-fourth of the Presidium at "regular elections" is enjoined by the 1961 statute,[22] a dominant faction will now find it easier to eliminate its opponents. If the factions are relatively equal

[21] In the Stalin succession not a single Presidium member, except Beria, was removed for four years.

[22] These are presumably the elections that occur after a Party Congress; recalcitrant Presidium members are still of course subject to removal between Congresses.

in strength, however, this provision could exacerbate conflict instead of reducing it, contrary to Khrushchev's intention. Khrushchev, then, apparently intended the Party machine to rule, but believed that to do so it had to be led by a personal ruler. He and his partisans made much of the obstruction to his proposals offered by the post-Stalin Presidium, and he seemed determined to obviate this for his successor. The powers he had secured for himself were not to lapse when he left the political scene or be arrogated by the newly constituted Presidium, which is the most suitable existing body for oligarchical rule. They were to pass to his successor, so that he in turn could effectively govern the Party machine.

THE PERSONALITY PROBLEM

The distribution of power and authority among the leaders, no less than the arrangement of institutions and leading bodies, must be properly arranged if there is to be an orderly transfer of dictatorial power. Khrushchev dealt with this double problem by trying to assure that the Party machine, its sovereignty firmly established, would pass at the decisive moment to the personal control of an heir presumptive. Until then, the various parts of the machine were arranged so that only Khrushchev would command them all; the heir was meant to gain a personal ascendancy at the critical moment, comparable to that once possessed by Khrushchev.

In deliberating on personnel arrangements for the succession, Khrushchev was limited to the material at hand, to the men through whom he had exercised his power. Whatever their true capacities, few of them have had long experience in managing the Soviet system from its center. Although Stalin may have denigrated his lieutenants as mere pygmies, there were nonetheless highly experienced men among them who for decades had been close to the centers of power. Denied the glorification which Stalin exacted for himself, they were yet able to bask in his reflected glory, and thus to acquire a mystique of their own. Western leaders who dealt with them were not contemptuous, but saw important political qualities in these men. The same had been true of Lenin's chief lieutenants when illness ended his rule. Although overshadowed by the founder of the Communist Party and state, they had had the chance to learn from his political genius, having served as his principal instruments in the supreme political acts of executing a revolution and establishing a new regime.

It is different with the men who were around Khrushchev. Few have had experience in the top leadership extending beyond Khrushchev's own period of rule: only Mikoyan, Kosygin, Suslov, and Shvernik held high posts under Stalin for any length of time. Moreover, while the top leadership was, on the whole, surprisingly stable under Stalin, under Khrushchev it was not. Of the men who rose to power with Stalin in the 1920s, around half remained on the Politburo for four or more years until the great purge, while the other half stayed in power until Stalin's death almost two decades later.[23] Khrushchev, on the other hand, ruled by rotation: of the fifteen persons elected to the Presidium in June, 1957, when Khrushchev seized power, only Khrushchev and four others were still active

[23] There are two exceptions: Kalinin died before Stalin, and A. A. Andreev was demoted a few months before Stalin's death.

members in October, 1964, when he was overthrown. These four, Mikoyan, Suslov, Brezhnev, and Shvernik, were outnumbered by the five men who were appointed from 1960 to 1962 (Podgorny, Polyansky, Kosygin, Voronov, and Kirilenko). The reason for this rapid turnover is to be sought in Khrushchev's mode of rule. Since he could not terrorize his principal aides, he relied on rotation to make them insecure and to prevent them from establishing secure personal bases of power.

It might be supposed that a policy of rotation, while it deprives most of his lieutenants of prolonged and rich political experience, increases the likelihood that men of high caliber will rise to the top. The men Khrushchev brought into the leadership, however, appear to lack the exceptional qualities that enable a man to dominate a great state, although it may yet turn out that there is one or more among them who possesses the requisite intellect and overpowering will, but who has been prevented from displaying them to the world, just as Khrushchev was unable to display these qualities while Stalin lived. In any case the presence of numerous leaders possessed of outstanding qualities is not required for an orderly succession, and is probably even incompatible with it. The optimum number is one.

Khrushchev encountered the succession problem almost at the moment of his acquisition of dictatorial power, since he was already sixty-three years old. At the same time, he had to consolidate his rule, which was subject to new challenges. Faced with this double difficulty, Khrushchev naturally slighted the succession problem in his initial dispositions. To supervise the Party machine, the most powerful agency of his rule, he chose Kirichenko, whose Ukrainian origins and limited political experience, almost all of it in the Ukraine, probably made him a doubtful candidate for the succession at that time. In this early period, the chief counterweights to Kirichenko's power, designed to prevent its aggrandizement, appeared to be Aristov and Kozlov. Aristov had special responsibility for the part of the Party machine that lay in the Russian Republic, while Kozlov was Khrushchev's chief deputy in the government. The circumstances surrounding Kirichenko's fall from grace in 1959 are clouded, but there is reason to believe that he may have overreached himself in the exercise of his great powers.

Khrushchev's new arrangements, which took form in the first half of 1960, showed a somewhat greater concern for the personality aspect of the succession problem, and he began to lean towards the Leningrad organization instead of to the Ukrainian as heretofore. In Kirichenko's place now appeared a highly eligible candidate for the succession, Frol Kozlov, who was transferred from the government to the Party Secretariat. As noted earlier, Kozlov's remarkable rise after November, 1953, was probably due to Khrushchev. He subsequently reported in Khrushchev's stead to the Central Committee on the Bucharest meeting of Communist leaders in June, 1960, a crucial event in the developing Sino-Soviet polemic. At the XXII Party Congress, Kozlov, in presenting "Amendments to the Statute" of the CPSU, followed in the footsteps of Khrushchev, who performed that same role at the XIX Party Congress (1952). Moreover, Kozlov was presiding officer at the opening session of the Congress.[24] Following the XXII Congress, the new Central Committee elected a Secretariat in which Kozlov's name followed Khrushchev's; the other Secretaries were listed alphabetically. These signs of Kozlov's rising authority could have meant that he was Khrushchev's presumptive successor.

Lacking Stalin's vast powers, however, Khrushchev was unwilling to give Kozlov as much authority as Malenkov had had under Stalin. On entering the Party Secretariat, Kozlov gave up his government post, unlike Malenkov, who did not cease to be Deputy Chairman of the Council of Ministers when he became Secretary of the Central Committee in 1948. Kozlov was left off the Bureau for the Russian Republic, which limited his authority over an important segment of the Party machine. Moreover, he was not accorded a special title to designate his position as second among the Secretaries. The power of strong rivals was set against Kozlov's to balance and circumscribe it. As counterpoise to Kozlov's power in the Secretariat, successive *apparatchiks* were made ascendant in the Bureau for the Russian Republic, of which Kozlov was not even a member: first Aristov, then Voronov, finally Kirilenko. In the state-government bureaucracy, Kozlov's power was balanced by that of Brezhnev, Mikoyan, and Kosygin, in the Secretariat, by that of Suslov.

When he enhanced Kozlov's position, Khrushchev took care to strengthen his own, as Stalin had done in 1952. Under the new dispensation, he alone was a member of all

[24] The presiding officers at the openings of recent Congresses have been Molotov (XIX), Bulganin (XX), Kirichenko (XXI), and Kozlov (XXII). Thus, the opening session of the next, due to convene by October, 1965, may also be presided over by the second-ranking leader, whoever he may be.

the top organs of dictatorship: the Presidium, the Secretariat of the Central Committee, the Central Committee's Bureau for the Russian Republic, and the USSR Council of Ministers. The other leaders sat on no more than two of these four bodies. At the January, 1961, plenum of the Central Committee, Khrushchev forcefully asserted his authority over the speakers, not excepting Presidium members. The cult of Khrushchev, a potent instrument of personal rule and one that had grown appreciably since 1957, received fresh impetus. According to the Central Committee (Resolution of June 30, 1956), "any action against" Stalin was ruled out during his lifetime because of his personality cult, which guaranteed him public support; Khrushchev, too, used the cult of his person to deter political opposition. He may even have placed too great a reliance on it.

Kozlov's health was brought in question in the spring of 1961 when he suffered a heart attack. Even so, his authority continued to rise afterwards, reaching a high point at the XXII Party Congress in October, 1961, and in the following months. He personally conducted several purges in the minority republics, and even acted on occasion as a trouble-shooter in the Russian Republic. Subsequently, in the fall of 1962, his preeminent position among Khrushchev's lieutenants became less certain. In November, the Party was radically reorganized in ways that had not been foreshadowed in his report the previous year on the new Party statute, or in his various articles on Party organization. So far as is known, he played no special role in implementing the reorganization. In the spring of 1963 Kozlov had a second heart attack, the effect of which was to deprive him of his former status as heir presumptive.

As a result, the question of Khrushchev's personnel arrangements for the succession was reopened.

In June, 1963, Khrushchev made new arrangements for the succession. Leonid Brezhnev, then the nominal head of state (Chairman of the Presidium of the Supreme Soviet), was returned to the Secretariat of the Central Committee after a three years' absence. His renewed place at the key center of power and the wide experience he had acquired in special assignments for Khrushchev made it appear that he had replaced Kozlov as heir presumptive.

The same plenum of the Central Committee that elected Brezhnev to the Secretariat also elected Nikolai Podgorny to that body, transferring him from the Ukraine, where he headed the Party organization. The parallel with Khrushchev's move to Moscow in 1949 is striking. Just as Stalin brought Khrushchev into the Secretariat to balance the power acquired by Malenkov after Zhdanov's death, so Khrushchev brought Podgorny into the Secretariat to balance Brezhnev's newly granted power following Kozlov's severe illness. A new triad took shape, with Khrushchev, the dictator; Brezhnev, the heir presumptive; and Podgorny, the counter heir. At the same time, Khrushchev left both men out of the Bureau for the Russian Republic, in which a fourth key figure, A. Kirilenko, remained the only full Presidium member besides Khrushchev himself. Thus, for the first time, Khrushchev strongly committed himself to a single provincial organization, the Ukrainian, in which Brezhnev, Podgorny, and Kirilenko originated.[25]

In the assignment of powers and offices to the heir pre-

[25] See Chapter VIII for a further, more detailed discussion of this situation.

sumptive, a crucial consideration is the mechanism by which he is to seize power at the decisive moment. In Stalin's arrangements, evidently Malenkov, who, apart from Stalin, was the only member of all three top bodies (Presidium, Secretariat, and Council of Ministers), was somehow to make himself head of these bodies when Stalin died. By reforming the institutions of rule, however, Khrushchev altered the problem of devising a mechanism for transferring the ruler's power to his successor. As noted earlier, while Khrushchev made the sovereignty of the Party machine the key to an orderly succession, he at the same time created important divisions in the Party machine in an effort to assure the implementation of his will and to forestall efforts to limit his power. These divisions were of various kinds. The staff of the central organs were split geographically into a Russian and a non-Russian part.[26] Except for Khrushchev, no Secretary of the Central Committee sat on the Russian Bureau after 1960. Other central bureaus were established for related republics (e.g., in Central Asia) in late 1962. The central staff was divided functionally into bureaus and commissions for agriculture, industry, ideology, Party organs (including cadres), and Party-state control. These divisions were not established simply to increase the efficiency of Party rule, although this was surely one of their chief purposes. They also served a more narrowly political aim: they were headed by Party Secretaries and established a balance between them. The increase in the number of Secretaries, from five to nine in October, 1961, and from nine to four-

[26] Cf. Central Committee Decree of March 14, 1956, *Spravochnik Partiinogo Rabotnika* (Handbook for Party Workers) (Moscow, Gospolitizdat, 1957), p. 127.

teen in November, 1962, although this may have increased the overall power of the Secretariat, tended to fragment it.

Khrushchev may have intended subsequently to reintegrate the Secretariat and to concentrate a large part of its substantial powers in the hands of a firmly designated heir presumptive. Such an arrangement, however, manifestly would have involved an appreciable threat to his own rule. Lacking confidence in the security of his own position even after seven years of rule, Khrushchev was unwilling to grant such powers to a *presumptive* heir, but *possible* rival. As a result, when he was overthrown, contenders for the succession faced the crucial task of reintegrating the Secretariat and establishing personal control over it in order to make good their claims to rule.

VII: The Prospects—Organs and Institutions

Khrushchev was relieved of his high posts in the Party and government at his "request" on October 14, 1964.[1] Thus began the Khrushchev succession, the third in Soviet history. While we cannot know its outcome in advance, it is possible to consider, in general terms and conditionally, what may follow Khrushchev's passing from the political scene. We can discuss the forms and foci of conflict, the issues that are likely to arise, and the ways in which they might be resolved; we can discuss the principal candidates, in so far as they have presently emerged; we can examine the critical junctures in the succession, the turning points that may determine for a time the internal development of the USSR—although we cannot predict which way the turn will go.

In what follows, the term "phases" is used, and perhaps something should be said of what we mean by the term. Phases in the succession are not disparate things, but successive developments that can be characterized by some distinguishing feature. The first phase is characterized by the distribution of the former ruler's powers and by the

[1] *Pravda,* October 16, 1964.

unsettling circumstance that an individual may try to arrogate much of it to himself. The second phase—if there is one—is the phase of shared power, or oligarchy; it is an *unstable* oligarchy, in which the threat of a new bid for individual rule remains. There may be a third phase in which a new ruler consolidates his power, but it would depend so much on what had gone before that it will not concern us much here.

FIRST PHASE

In the first days of the succession, Khrushchev's heirs had to effect at least a provisional redistribution of his great powers, and this seems certain to produce a serious confrontation of the chief groups in higher Soviet politics. This phase of the succession is crucial. It provides a fleeting opportunity for a quick resolution of the problem if the heir presumptive, or some other would-be dictator, can establish the basis for a stable system of personal rule. In 1953, Malenkov moved quickly to try to establish himself as Stalin's successor, but his effort was blocked. In the first phase of the Lenin succession, no such attempt was made, chiefly because Lenin's power was so firmly founded in his personal qualities that a new basis of power had to be created, for which Stalin required several years. In the first days of the Khrushchev succession, Brezhnev was able to make himself First Secretary of the Central Committee. He immediately attempted to consolidate his position by arrogating to himself as much of Khrushchev's power as possible. As heir presumptive he was in the most favorable position to establish himself as Khrushchev's successor. Yet the obstacles he faced were formidable.

Khrushchev's powers inhered in a set of offices, titles, institutional forms, and rituals. To acquire most of Khrushchev's former powers, Brezhnev, or any other contender, would probably need to make himself head of the government (Chairman of the Council of Ministers) as well as Party head—more precisely First Secretary of the Central Committee. In opposition to his designs, however, a strong effort will probably be made to maintain the separation of these posts, as was done after Stalin's death. Such a separation was effected on March 14, 1953, when "a plenum of the Central Committee," or rather a small group acting in its name, granted "the request of the Chairman of the Council of Ministers of the USSR, Comrade G. M. Malenkov, to be released from the duties of Secretary of the Central Committee of the CPSU." [2] There was a week's delay in announcing this change, which suggests the kind of struggle that was waged over it. A similar division was effected in Czechoslovakia very shortly afterwards, following the death of Klement Gottwald on March 14. This division of posts was then imposed upon Hungary, where Mátyás Rákosi gave up his position as head of the government in order to strengthen "collective leadership" (July 2). Subsequently it was adopted in the satellites of Poland, East Germany, Rumania, Bulgaria, and Albania.

Against this precedent, a candidate for the Khrushchev succession might cite Khrushchev's example after 1958, when he united the two posts in his own person. There was a certain defensiveness about this, however. In his speech nominating Khrushchev to head the government, Voroshilov announced that "the Central Committee has

[2] *Pravda*, March 21, 1953.

decided that Comrade Nikita Sergeyevich Khrushchev is to remain in the post of First Secretary of the Central Committee"—as though otherwise he would have been expected to give it up on becoming head of the government.[3] Whether Khrushchev's joint occupancy of the two posts for the better part of a decade will efface the earlier determination to prevent this is hard to know. In any case, while historical precedents doubtless play a part in these matters, what will be decisive is the support that can be mustered against the almost certain opposition of Khrushchev's other heirs. When Khrushchev was overthrown, the posts were divided between Brezhnev and Alexei Kosygin, giving critical importance to the question of the relations between the two leaders. In the first years after Stalin's death, the sharpest personal rivalry was between the head of the government (Malenkov) and the *de facto* head of the Party (Khrushchev); this was also true in Hungary and, in less degree, in Bulgaria. Elsewhere, however, one of the two men was the supreme leader and the other clearly his subordinate. This pattern was first established by Stalin in 1930 when he placed his lieutenant, Molotov, at the head of the government. It has certain advantages, although Khrushchev's experience with Bulganin (an early ally who later secretly joined his opponents) suggests the dangers in such an arrangement. Moreover, it has the disadvantage of being based on a Stalinist precedent (1930–1941); here a contender for the succession faces a dilemma, however, since *combining* the two posts in the person of the ruler is also based on a Stalinist precedent (1941–1953). Nevertheless, to allay opposition, Brezhnev, the dominant figure in the first phase

[3] *Pravda,* March 28, 1958.

of the succession, may be content, at least for a time, to secure the post of First Secretary for himself while attempting to place a trusted ally or a figurehead at the head of the government. (Whether Kosygin is the one or the other remains to be seen.) If Brezhnev lacks a strong basis of support in the government, his opponents may try to strengthen the government bureaucracy, both as an instrument of rule and of factional struggle.

In considering the scramble for supreme office at the outset of the succession, it is necessary to recall that there are important differences between the two top posts, the one in the government, and the other in the Party. The post of Chairman of the Council of Ministers (or, as it was formerly, Council of People's Commissars), is both a constitutional and a traditional office. Lenin and Stalin both occupied it at the time of their death, and in each instance their heirs had to find a replacement. Khrushchev too had to be replaced in the post; there was no necessity, however, to replace him as First Secretary of the Central Committee. The position is nowhere mentioned in the Party statute, and there is, in fact, no precedent for appointing a head of the Secretariat at the time of the dictator's political demise. When Lenin fell ill, Stalin already was "General Secretary of the C.C.," although it was several years before it came to signify that he was head of the Party.[4]

After the great purge of the 1930s, Stalin's title of General Secretary fell into disuse. It was unmentioned in eulogies and commentary on his death, and none of his heirs received it. Six months passed before Khrushchev was elected "first" Secretary of the Central Committee.

[4] Stalin was confirmed in the post, however, when the XIII Party Congress met a few months after Lenin's death (see Chapter III).

In view of this absence of continuity in the office, it is evident that it did not simply fall empty when Khrushchev vacated it. No doubt Brezhnev's success in immediately being appointed First Secretary was partly due to a desire to display continuity of leadership; nevertheless it implies the possession of an impressive degree of power at the moment of Khrushchev's overthrow.[5]

Although he was quickly designated First Secretary of the Central Committee, this did not necessarily give Brezhnev control of the entire Party apparatus. Because of Khrushchev's innovations, the part of the central Party apparatus that deals with the Russian Republic evidently is subordinate to the Russian Bureau, not to the Secretariat. Thus, to gain full control over the Party apparatus in the largest republic in the USSR, with more than half the country's population, Brezhnev, or some subsequent candidate for the succession, would presumably require the office of Chairman of the Russian Bureau. Alternatively, he could try to undo Khrushchev's division of the central Party apparatus, but this might take time to bring about. In brief, because Khrushchev divided and subdivided the regime's power to assure his personal rule, a successor will have to reassemble this power and unite it in his own person. He will find this difficult to accomplish quickly in face of opposition from his colleagues.

Apart from the distribution of Khrushchev's powers among his erstwhile lieutenants, a critical question will

[5] Khrushchev's title later became "First Secretary" in order to distinguish him from the many provincial "first" Secretaries on all levels of the Party apparatus. In this book, the title has generally appeared as "First Secretary" to conform to normal English usage; but in the USSR the distinction is preserved, so that the senior secretary in the Central Committee is the "First Secretary," but in all other Party committees he is the "first" Secretary.

be the future composition of the key bodies of the Central Committee: the Presidium, the Secretariat, and the Russian Bureau. The initial contention may be most acute over the choice of members for the Secretariat and the Russian Bureau, since these are the decisive levers in the Party apparatus. However, the Party Presidium, with Khrushchev no longer able to dominate policy-making and to arbitrate factional disputes, may regain, at least for a time, some of its statutory authority as the policy-making body between plenary meetings of the Central Committee.[6] Thus there may be renewed contention on the issue of whether the Secretaries (and perhaps the Russian Bureau members) should be *ex officio* members of the Presidium. After Khrushchev established his ascendancy in 1957, one of the means he used to make the Party machine sovereign over the other instruments of rule was to enlarge the Secretariat and place *all* its members on the Presidium. Stalin had established a precedent for this at the time of the XIX Party Congress (1952). This practice has some basis, by analogy, in the Party statute, which makes territorial Secretaries (though not central Secretaries) members of the corresponding bureau. Following the XXII Congress in 1961, however, when Khrushchev was dividing the instruments of his rule in order to enhance his personal control over them, most of the Secretaries then chosen were left off the Presidium. This meant that, while they had access to important levers of the Party's organizational machinery, they were cut off from direct influence on the large issues of national policy.

The question of restoring central Secretaries to the

[6] Plenary meetings are required by the statute at least once every six months.

Presidium may become a contentious issue in the initial phase of the succession. A leader, or a faction, that is strong in the Secretariat will try to increase its representation in the Presidium in order to gain a dominant voice in policy-making. His opponents in the Presidium, on the other hand, will want to gain representation in the Secretariat for themselves. In the two previous successions, Stalin and Khrushchev were the sole Presidium members in the Secretariat, while their principal opponents were kept off it. In the initial phase of the Khrushchev succession Suslov and Podgorny remained on the Secretariat along with Brezhnev, possibly limiting his freedom of action.

The extent of changes in the leading bodies that will result from the initial confrontation following Khrushchev's overthrow is difficult to predict. After Lenin's incapacitation, and again after his death, only small changes were made in their membership. The important shifts of power occurred *within* the Politburo. On the other hand, when Stalin died, the Party Presidium and the government were largely reconstituted. Since Khrushchev's will has been decisive in determining the membership of the leading bodies, his departure from the scene could lead to substantial early changes. The confrontation in the first days of the succession will lead to reappraisals of the strengths of the various factions and institutions in the new circumstance of Khrushchev's absence. As a result, their representation in the leading Party bodies could be significantly altered.

At the time Khrushchev was overthrown no other change was made in the regime's leading bodies, presumably because the leaders of the coup sought to give an impression of continuity in the leadership. Nevertheless, large changes in the composition of the leading bodies may not be long in coming.

SECOND PHASE

The initial phase of succession will leave its mark in various ways, strongly coloring the next phase of succession. This will be especially true if, as may happen, it is focused on an unsuccessful bid for individual rule. If such a bid is made by a leader with strong personal qualities, the coalition that defeated him would tend to cohere out of a concern that he might try again. If his initial bid were defeated by a relatively narrow margin, he might even be able to share power with his opponents for a time, as Malenkov did after 1953. On the other hand, if he suffered strong defeat, he might be excluded from the ruling group, as Trotsky was within a few months of Lenin's illness. For, although Trotsky remained a member of the Politburo, he had little power within it.

In any case, an unsuccessful attempt to establish individual rule would be followed by a temporary accommodation among the most powerful leaders, an oligarchical arrangement that would be presented to the world as a new "collective leadership" based on Lenin's principles of Party life. If the succession enters this new, less acute, phase, factions will be established on a more permanent basis, the lines of struggle will be demarcated, and personal strategies will be elaborated and efforts made to implement them. While the Secretariat and the Bureau for the Russian Republic may be the chief battlegrounds in the first, acute phase, the Presidium is likely to become the organ of oligarchical rule in the next phase, which conceivably might last for several years.

If there is to be oligarchical rule in the USSR, it is not likely to be rule by the Central Committee, but rather by a small group within it. The Presidium of the Central Committee provided a natural basis for oligarchy in the two previous successions, while the Secretariat provided the basis for individual rule. The Presidium is about the right size, usually varying from ten to fifteen members, while the parent body is more than twenty times as large. Moreover, the Presidium has both traditional and statutory authority.

It will be more difficult to make the Presidium the basis for oligarchy in the Khrushchev succession, however, because of a previously noted statutory change. Now at least one-fourth of its membership must be newly elected—this is a *minimum* requirement—and members are normally limited to three terms, i.e., a maximum of twelve years. Since this provision is designed to facilitate individual rule, it would probably have to be amended or ignored (either, of course, is quite possible), before the Presidium could become a stable oligarchical body. Moreover, stability of the Presidium is a necessary, not a sufficient, condition for oligarchy.

Even a stable Presidium, in which the members are accorded long tenure, need not mean that the oligarchy based on it is also stable. In both the Lenin and the Stalin successions, the Presidium (Politburo) changed very little in the first four years, yet during this time the oligarchy based on it was being effectively undermined by the future ruler. This was possible because an oligarchy based on the Presidium has a second vulnerable point. A dominant leader (or faction) can use the Secretariat to deprive the Presidium as a collective body, of its policy-making prerogatives. Unless the post-Khrushchev Presidium succeeds, for the first time in Soviet history, in controlling the Secretariat and its members, it will find it difficult to preserve its stability and its prerogatives and will probably fail as an oligarchical body.

What of the Central Committee? Will it become the arbiter of struggles within the central apparatus, thereby establishing its own supremacy? While the Central Committee is charged by the statute with electing its leading personnel, including a head of the Secretariat if it so wishes, the actual decisions almost certainly will be made by a small group within it, as a result of bargaining. The results, of course, will be issued in the name of the Central Committee, like all major decisions.

It is true that Khrushchev used the Central Committee not long ago in his rise to power and may thereby have conferred a modicum of authority and prestige on that body that has persisted. But Khrushchev did not defer to it after 1957, and took measures to weaken its capacity to intervene as a corporate body in high politics.

Basically, the Central Committee is an assembly of officeholders, 330 of them, most of whom are dependent on patrons. When dispersed, as they are between plenums, the members have no way of organizing discussion of the leadership's actions. "Factionalism," it will be recalled, is formally banned. Even when assembled, the Central Committee is too unwieldy a body to constitute an effective arbiter of differences within the top leadership. While succession crises, especially when prolonged, have increased the political importance of the Central Committee, this importance has not come about because the Central Committee resolved to exercise its statutory rights, but rather because the dominant faction chose to use it to destroy the opposing faction. The role played by the 330-man Central Committee in the overthrow of Khrushchev is at least questionable.

The Central Committee is better suited for manipulation by the chief protagonists than for playing an independent role. Lacking a well-established constitution and set of procedures, it is a highly variable institution. There is no definite time for meetings, so the members can assemble only when summoned. Its membership is not fixed, but tends to grow by leaps and bounds. While numerous positions in the Soviet system confer *ex officio* membership in the Central Committee by custom, many do not, so that institutional representation in the Central Committee is itself a key issue of Soviet politics.

The Central Committee may sit by itself, or with numerous experts present, or together with the revision commission. Its meetings are not always announced in advance and therefore can be retroactively fabricated, as evidently happened in March and April of 1953 and perhaps again on October 14, 1964, when a plenum of the Central Committee is supposed to have replaced Khrushchev with Brezhnev. Once a meeting has been announced, the leaders can readily postpone it if they wish to. Its proceedings may be published in full, in part, or not published at all. Its agenda varies widely, not only from meeting to meeting, but from year to year. The determination of these matters does not lie within the capacity of this unwieldy body, but must be made for it by a small executive group, which thereby controls it.

We conclude from this that the Central Committee cannot be supreme in the Soviet system of rule, nor is it likely to become an autonomously decisive body. This is not to deny it an important role in the succession, however, as we shall have occasion to observe in what follows.

INSTITUTIONAL RIVALRY

Departure of the ruler leads to intensified factional conflict among the top leaders. These factions correspond in some measure to functional and territorial divisions in the leadership. Initially, if the Khrushchev succession is waged within the central Party apparatus, the rival groupings will represent divisions of the Party machine. As struggle in the Presidium is sharpened, however, institutional struggle may become an important, perhaps crucial, aspect. Subsequent politicking may be restricted to the bargaining and maneuvering of leaders of the Party machine, the government bureaucracy, and other institutions. With the passage of time, however, if the succession is not resolved, the political arena inevitably is enlarged.

Within the Presidium, the chief institutions traditionally represented are the central Party apparatus, the central government, and certain territorial organizations, usually the Ukrainian and the Russian. At the time of Khrushchev's overthrow, the division of full Presidium members (apart from Khrushchev) was as follows: central Party apparatus—Brezhnev, Podgorny, Suslov, Shvernik, and Kozlov (who remained inactive because of illness); central state and government—Mikoyan, Kosygin, and Polyansky; territorial—the Russian Republic was represented by its head of government, Voronov, and by the leading figure in its Party apparatus, Kirilenko. From this it is apparent that after 1957, when Khrushchev largely deprived the government apparatus of its representation in the Presidium while greatly increasing that of the Party machine, he went far to restore the balance between them. While this balance was preserved in the initial dispositions after Khrushchev's overthrow, it may become a crucial issue in the future maneuvering of his heirs. Leaders of the Party machine may try to alter the Presidium's membership in their favor, although this may be difficult unless they can reach a limited accommodation among themselves. In any case, the succession may enter a second phase of unstable oligarchical rule with the government bureaucracy well represented in the Presidium, along with the chief divisions of the Party apparatus.

If the succession continues for some time, the Presidium probably will be unable to contain the struggle, which will spread to a wider arena, most likely to the parent body, the Central Committee. In the past, as we have emphasized, the Central Committee has been drawn into the succession by a small group with the aim of subverting the Presidium. Yet precisely because of the great size that makes it so unwieldy, the Central Committee is far more representative than the Presidium of the diverse institutional and functional groupings in the leadership.

The professional officers of the armed forces, for example, have only once and very briefly had a representative in the Presidium (in the person of Marshal Zhukov), but they have numerous representatives in the Central Committee. Moreover, under conditions of individual rule like that exercised by Khrushchev from 1957 to 1964, Presidium members tended to become personal agents of

Khrushchev's rule; only secondarily and in an attenuated sense were they representatives of the institutions in which they worked, although with Khrushchev's removal their attachment to these institutions necessarily increased.

Central Committee members, however, have closer ties with particular institutions. While the difference is one of degree, it might acquire considerable significance in the succession, particularly if it were prolonged. Plenums of the Central Committee are not suitable for legislative deliberations, but they could become forums in which the diverse views of professional and functional groups gain expression, with the further consequence, perhaps, that informal alliances between these interest groups might be formed outside the precincts of the Central Committee.[7] Interest groups in the USSR, to revert to a point made earlier, are not "pressure groups" such as exist in the Western democracies. Their political significance for the most part stems from their influence in *institutions.*

Institutional conflict as a general feature of the Soviet system has already been discussed (see Chapter IV). It will suffice here, therefore, to consider how developments since 1958 may affect such conflict during the Khrushchev succession.

The state bureaucracy's representation in the Presidium was increased during the last years of Khrushchev's rule, presumably with the object of improving the Presidium's capacity to deliberate on questions of policy, yet on the

7 Even if the Central Committee did become such a forum, however, it probably would still lack the capacity to decide the succession: either the contending factions in its executive organs would maintain their control over the Central Committee, or the arena of struggle would be widened to include groups standing outside the Central Committee.

whole the bureaucracy was subordinated even further to the Party apparatus. Because of its functional importance for the efficient working of the economy, the state bureaucracy will probably acquire a greater voice in policy-making during the Khrushchev succession. However, unless there is a fundamental realignment of political forces in the Soviet system, any such gains might be transitory. As noted earlier, a lasting improvement in the bureaucracy's political power probably requires formation of an alliance with other institutions in order to overthrow the supremacy of the Party machine.

Under Khrushchev the Party machine was so overloaded with diverse and somewhat contradictory responsibilities that some observers believe it may simply fall from its own weight. This seems doubtful; yet the strains placed upon the Party apparatus are so great, and it has been so much diluted by experts and administrators, that it would be no less an error to suppose it to be invulnerable. It might fall victim to its political enemies within the Communist Party during the succession, if they could unite against it. The key political struggle may be between the Party apparatus and the state bureaucracy, but the latter needs allies to win.

The military will certainly have a role in the Khrushchev succession crisis, but assessing its political potential is complicated by a number of factors. The present top military leaders, although they personally benefited greatly from Khrushchev's favor, showed signs of restiveness at his assumption of a decisive role in the evolution of Soviet military doctrine and force posture, and his subjection of the military forces to an intricate system of controls by the

Party machine. They may try to capitalize on the Khrushchev succession to win back at least the relative autonomy they had won during the Stalin succession.

The military chiefs have never been an independent force in Soviet politics, however, and their most likely role now is as an ally of a faction in the Party leadership. They, or their successors, may support the leaders of the Party machine, especially if they are promised increased funds for defense. Such an alliance might lessen the succession crisis by helping the Party machine gain an early victory, although the benefits received by the military establishment from such a victory might in the end prove disappointing.

Another kind of alliance may be open to the military chiefs, however. As noted above, they may associate themselves with the leaders of other institutions now controlled by the Party machine, in an alliance directed against that machine. Perhaps only by such an alliance could the military establishment rid itself of the close Party (and political police) control to which it is now subject and achieve an independent voice in military matters comparable to that of defense chiefs in the West.

The current defense chiefs may not be well qualified to conduct the struggle for autonomy. They have less popular renown for exploits in World War II than did the comparable group of defense officials at the time of Stalin's death. They are now older, include a disproportionate number of Ukrainians, and were obviously beneficiaries of Khrushchev's political favor. These circumstances could make them vulnerable to a hostile political leadership.

Weapons developments of the past decade have posed the problem of the military's autonomy in a new and acute form. With the removal of Khrushchev, command and control of the armed forces, and particularly of the strategic forces, has become a sensitive question for the leadership. One possible solution is to transfer, from the political to the military leadership, the authority to *alert* the strategic nuclear forces in an emergency. (It is most unlikely that the military chiefs would ever be given discretionary authority to *launch* the strategic forces.) This solution would run strongly counter to Soviet traditions, however, and may be particularly unwelcome to the Party leaders as an interim measure during a period of political instability. Yet the alternative may be to retain this authority within a divided political leadership, thus degrading the capacity of the Soviet strategic forces to act quickly in an emergency.

The dilemma points up a crucial problem for Khrushchev's heirs. While each faction will probably try to win over the military hierarchy, or at least important elements in it, success in the competition may require making large promises or serious concessions. Promises, of course, can be broken, but this is a lesson that may still be fresh in the minds of the marshals, for Khrushchev employed such tactics in his rise to power. On the other hand, real concessions, particularly such as granting the military increased autonomy in control over the strategic forces, may seem too high a price to pay.

The ongoing revolution in weaponry has also tended to intensify conflicts among branches of the military establishment. The traditional branches have suffered at the hands of the politicians (under Khrushchev, certainly, if not under Stalin), and their decline has clearly been resented by the men who head them. Those who command the most modern arms are also not without grievances. While the USSR has astounded the world by its rapid development of new strategic weapons systems, in several instances the political leadership has been slow to convert these technological breakthroughs into sizable operational forces. Thus the various branches of the military establishment have strong motives for trying to influence the future decisions that will affect them. This may bring the military into the political arena arrayed in contending factions, however, and not as a unified force. Thus while divisions increase the likelihood that military leaders will take an active part in the succession struggle, they reduce their probable effectiveness.

By his role in the Stalin succession, Marshal Zhukov, a lifetime soldier, established a precedent where previously there was none. Its effect on future successions, and in particular on the Khrushchev succession, is hard to gauge. Zhukov succeeded in winning a considerable measure of autonomy from the Party's control agencies, if we can believe what the XXII Congress was told by Marshal Golikov, the man charged with restoring Party control:

> How serious the situation was was apparent from the extent to which the role of the military councils, political agencies, and Party organizations had been undermined and deprived of vitality; Party criticism of shortcomings in the conduct and the work of Communist commanders of all grades was forbidden in the army; one-man leadership had been detached from its Party basis . . . dissension between commanding officers and political agencies was cultivated. Party life and the work of the political agencies were subjected to bureaucratic direction and were reduced to narrow educational activity. The main political administration was slighted and downgraded. The manners of the petty tyrant were permitted in military research. Attempts were made to evade, in one way or

another, control by the Central Committee, to undermine the influence of the Party and to cut the army and navy off from the Party and the people. A cult of Zhukov's person was created. There was a growing drift to unlimited authority in the army and the country.[8]

Zhukov's success in lessening Party control over the military, which was achieved in little over a year as the Stalin succession struggle rose to its climax, may encourage others to follow in his footsteps, although his precipitate decline in the second half of 1957 could have an opposite effect. Perhaps the key question is a pedagogical one: what have the military learned from the Zhukov affair? Are they now aware that their autonomy depends upon divisions in the political leadership? Do they now see a need to form an alliance against the Party machine?

The Zhukov affair may also have been instructive for others in the leadership, but for them, too, the lesson is ambiguous. Does it show that military leaders make ideal allies, since the concessions accorded them can so easily be taken away? Or does it suggest that there may be hidden dangers in letting military leaders engage in politics, since their appetite appears to be whetted, as Zhukov's was, by initial success?

If the military did succeed in increasing its influence on Soviet policy during the succession, how would that influence be used? First, no doubt, to increase military spending and to require more favorable terms in any arms control agreement with the West. Yet, at the same time, the military might also press for a more conservative for-

[8] Golikov's notion that the lessening of Party control removes the limits, or restraints, on authority is striking and has rarely been stated so baldly in the USSR. Golikov does not amplify his intriguing remark on the drift to unlimited authority in the country (*strane*). *XXII S"ezd KPSS* (Moscow, Gospolitizdat, 1962), III, 67.

eign policy toward the West, one more in accord with the military balance between the two sides.[9] The period from 1958 to 1962, when the USSR threatened the West's position in Berlin while neglecting to build up its intercontinental strategic forces, was one in which the military leadership probably was compelled to accept military and foreign policies that it did not like. Such an "adventurist" policy, at least, would be less likely in a period of increased military influence on the Soviet political leadership.

While the role played by Soviet military leaders in the Khrushchev succession doubtless will depend chiefly on internal developments, the state of tension in the world will affect the views and bargaining strength of both the military leaders and of those who seek their political support. For this as well as other reasons, the political leaders may prefer an initial period of quiescence in the Cold War.

Apart from its political potential, the military might be called upon to play a more direct and forceful role if a violent attempt were made to seize power. However, since violence played so small a part in the Stalin succession, when circumstances were more favorable to its employment, it seems unlikely that the Khrushchev succession will be marked by violence. In the event the military did intervene forcibly, it would probably be as the instrument of a political faction, not in a direct effort to seize power for itself.

The KGB (State Committee on Security) or political po-

[9] It is true that military considerations may lead to aggressive political moves that have the backing of military leaders, as in the Soviet placement of missiles in Cuba in 1962, but this is probably atypical and the Soviet military leadership may not have been unanimous in supporting the move.

lice, as it has been newly constituted in the post-Stalin era, will assuredly practice certain of its professional skills in the succession, those of political espionage if not those of the jailor. In retrospect, it appears that Khrushchev had considerable success in controlling the political police after 1953, and this may have played a greater role in his victory than is commonly supposed. Moreover, it is not unlikely that the political police played a part in Khrushchev's overthrow, and this conjecture, if widely made, will deepen the shadow cast by the KGB over Soviet politics. The question is not whether political espionage and coercion will be used, but rather how and by whom. Will the heads of the KGB succeed in placing it at the disposal of their political masters? Or will the KGB be effectively neutralized as an instrument of factional struggle, at least for a time?

Although the political police will be involved in the succession, because of its curtailed powers its role will be a restricted one. No contender is likely to make it the chief means in his bid for personal power, as Beria did in 1953. Thus a potentially disruptive factor in the succession has been removed and the chance of bloodshed reduced. This is not to say that a reduction in the role of the political police is the product of a secular trend that must continue. On the contrary, under certain circumstances, use of the political police as a means of repression might be intensified. It is not true, as Hitler proved, that police terror is incompatible with scientific-industrial progress; nor is even a libertarian society immune to its imposition. Moreover, Stalin's blood purge is not only a warning to those who would let themselves be tyrannized; it is also a model for a future tyrant, something Stalin lacked until Hitler showed him the way by his blood purge of the Nazi leadership in 1934.

While the present reduced role of the political police lessens the likelihood of violence in the aftermath of Khrushchev's political demise, it is not necessarily conducive to a more orderly succession. A key stabilizing factor that was present in the Stalin succession is now absent. The paralyzing fear of police-directed repression that the Soviet people experienced under Stalin persisted after his death. This terrible legacy may have given his heirs a needed period of grace in which to resolve the inevitable crisis produced by his death.

As fear abated, there were political stirrings, not only within the wide circle of Party leaders, but also among intellectuals and students. This development is described in an interview by David Burg, who experienced it while a student at Moscow University:

Burg: From 1951 to 1954, practically all of us showed to the world a completely straight Communist face. You confined any critical views of the regime to your closest friends and even then unpleasant things sometimes happened. The danger of arrest and deportation was immediate. I was, frankly, very surprised to learn in 1955 and 1956 after the "thaw" began, that there were a great number of other small circles of friends, thinking in much the same way, who had been cut off from each other.

Interviewer: How did you become aware of the "thaw"? Did it follow close after Stalin's death?

Burg: Not immediately—there was a short period of groping confusion. Then in the winter of '55 all of a sudden people started to talk about things they would never have mentioned previously. . . . And gradually there was more talk about politics, especially after the Twentieth Party Congress in 1956 when Khrushchev made his famous denunciation of Stalin.[10]

[10] "The Voice of a Dissenter," *Harper's Magazine* (May, 1961), p. 127.

Politically significant agitation then reached its height. The most critical period of the leadership struggle was the twenty months beginning with Khrushchev's attack on Stalin and ending with the purge of Zhukov. Subsequently, while fear of police repression declined further, the stabilization of Khrushchev's rule and the restoration of Party hegemony effectively discouraged widespread political dissidence or popular disaffection.[11]

Thus, in the decade since Stalin died, an easier and more permissive political atmosphere has evolved, in which defeated political opponents, while shorn of effective political power, are not, so far as we know, deprived of their lives. Political factions may now be protected by a powerful sanction: the initiator of more severe reprisals would be widely feared as an incipient Stalin, and his life might be imperiled along with his growing powers. For this reason, the political resolution of these groups may be substantially greater in the Khrushchev succession crisis than it was when Stalin died.

The effect of a curtailed political police power on the succession is thus likely to be ambivalent. While it reduces the likelihood of violence and bloodshed, it may encourage interest groups in the various non-Party institutions to participate in the higher politics of the regime. The alternative to a bloody succession, it must be emphasized, is not necessarily an orderly succession; the prospective absence of bloodshed may actually deepen the crisis by bringing into it many who otherwise would be deterred. The "normalization" of Soviet politics since Stalin, which has been widely noted in the West, may in certain circum-

[11] There have been occasional localized disturbances, however, such as the strikes and rioting in Kazakhstan in 1959.

stances produce not an orderly succession to Khrushchev but a deep crisis. For the principal measure of the depth of the Khrushchev succession crisis is not the number of those executed, but the effects of succession on Soviet institutions, and in particular on the hegemony of the Party machine.

VIII: The Prospects—Men and Issues

In the years after Khrushchev gained power in 1957 men from the Ukrainian Party organization became the dominant group in the leadership. These men were not Ukrainian nationalists, but Russified Ukrainians and Russians, much of whose lives had been spent in the Ukraine. For a time Khrushchev balanced their power in some measure by that of the Leningrad organization, and in somewhat less degree by the power of the Moscow provincial organization. After Kozlov's illness in mid-1963, however, the men from the Ukraine came to predominate. The suddenness of their rise in the past decade, and its close coincidence with Khrushchev's, are evident from some striking facts.

Seven of the seventeen Presidium members and candidates at the time of Khrushchev's ouster had not even been candidate members of the Central Committee elected in 1952: of these seven, five are from the Ukraine. Of the eleven full members of the Presidium, three entered the Central Committee before 1935 (Mikoyan, Shvernik, and Khrushchev), two in 1939 (Kosygin and Suslov), three in 1952 (Brezhnev, Kozlov, and Voronov);

but the remaining three were not even candidate members until 1956: Podgorny was fifty-two when he finally entered the Central Committee, Kirilenko, almost fifty, Polyansky, thirty-eight. All three started their careers in the Ukrainian Party organization when Khrushchev headed it (1938–1949). By 1962, a scant half dozen years after Khrushchev succeeded in bringing them into the Central Committee, he had further raised them to full membership in the Presidium. Two of the six candidate members under Khrushchev had worked in the Ukraine: Mzhavanadze entered the Central Committee only in 1956 (at the age of fifty-four); Shelest did not come into it until 1961.

Because Khrushchev had made them his deputies, the leaders from the Ukraine were close to the heart of power at the onset of the succession. As a result, their political and personal relations will influence its course and outcome, perhaps decisively. Are they a single bloc or faction, or are there divisions among them?

The key figures in Khrushchev's final succession arrangements, as noted before, were Brezhnev and Podgorny. Each is the center of a significant complex of personal ties, although it is difficult to establish their precise meaning. First, Brezhnev, and the men about him.

There is a remarkable association and parallelism between his career and that of Kirilenko, who was the only full member added to Khrushchev's Presidium after the XXII Congress (1961). Kirilenko is a Russian, despite his Ukrainian-sounding name.

Brezhnev and Kirilenko were born in the same year (1906) and joined the Party in the same year (1931). They received engineering training in their late twenties and worked in that field for a time. Both were suddenly promoted to "leading Party work" in the Ukraine in their early thirties, as a result of Stalin's blood purge. In 1938, when Khrushchev was rebuilding the Ukrainian Party machine, Brezhnev became a department head and subsequently a Secretary in the important Dnepropetrovsk oblast Party organization; Kirilenko became a Secretary, and then Second Secretary, in the neighboring oblast of Zaporozhe.[1] Thus, in 1941, when Nazi Germany attacked the USSR, Kirilenko had advanced about as far as Brezhnev. During the war the two men, then in their late thirties, engaged in Party work with armies in combat, although Kirilenko also worked for a time supervising military production as a plenipotentiary of the State Defense Committee.[2] In 1943 Kirilenko returned to his position as Second Secretary of the Zaporozhe *obkom* (oblast committee), which he continued to hold until 1947. In the last part of his tenure, however, he was subordinate to Brezhnev, who was brought into the *obkom* as the First Secretary. In 1947 both men were transferred to new posts in the Ukraine, Kirilenko becoming First Secretary of the Nicolaev oblast committee, Brezhnev, First Secretary of the key Dnepropetrovsk oblast committee.

In 1950, shortly after Khrushchev had moved from the Ukraine to Moscow to become a Secretary of the Central Committee, Brezhnev followed him there to work briefly in the apparatus of the Central Committee. That same

1 Stalino, where Khrushchev lived for a number of years and began his rise in the Party, is also close by.

2 The political significance of this assignment, if any, may stem from the hostility sometimes felt toward the State Defense Committee (which Stalin headed) by field commanders and the Party workers associated with them—men like Khrushchev, Bulganin, and Zhdanov.

year he was promoted to the post of First Secretary of the Central Committee of the Moldavian Republic. Thus Brezhnev, in his early forties, now moved well ahead of Kirilenko, who succeeded Brezhnev as First Secretary in Dnepropetrovsk in 1950 and held the post until 1955. At that time Khrushchev, who was extending his personal power into the Russian Republic, brought Kirilenko and a number of other Ukrainian provincial Party leaders into corresponding posts in Russia. Kirilenko was assigned to a major industrial city of the Urals, Sverdlovsk, where he remained until 1962.

After he moved to Moscow Brezhnev's fortunes became more closely involved in Moscow intrigues. His career reached a high point in 1952, at the XIX Congress, when he was brought back to Moscow as a Secretary of the Central Committee and a candidate member of Stalin's enlarged Presidium. He fell from this eminence when Stalin died, but subsequently Khrushchev's patronage raised him even higher, making him second only to Khrushchev himself. Kirilenko entered the Presidium as a candidate in 1957, lost this status in 1961 while still First Secretary in Sverdlovsk, but was raised to a still higher position in 1962. He was brought to Moscow, for the first time in his career, as Khrushchev's deputy in the Russian Bureau of the Central Committee, and full member of the Presidium.[3]

From this account of their careers, it seems clear that

[3] There is some mystery as to why Kirilenko lost his position as a candidate to the Presidium in October, 1961, only to be made a full member a few months later. The hypothesis that Kozlov caused his demotion and Khrushchev his subsequent promotion is questionable, since there was no evident change in Khrushchev's power during this brief interval of a few months.

Brezhnev and Kirilenko have both risen to leading positions as a result of Khrushchev's patronage, Brezhnev, however, being the favorite. What is less certain is the personal and political relation of the two men. The question is crucial for an understanding of Brezhnev's replacement of Khrushchev as First Secretary, as well as his future prospects in that office. If Kirilenko is an ally, Brezhnev's chances of gaining control of the Russian Bureau are enhanced; if not, he presents an obstacle to the consolidation of Brezhnev's power in the Party machine. Whatever their political relationship in the past, if the two men continue in their present positions, their future relations may significantly affect the course and outcome of the Khrushchev succession.

Several leaders in important posts have at times been associated with Kirilenko, although at present it is difficult to know whether their relation has been one of patronage, hostility, or indifference. Kirilenko was succeeded as Second Secretary of the Zaporozhe *obkom* by Georgi V. Yenyutin, who was brought there from a neighboring oblast. Now in his sixties, Yenyutin is Kirilenko's subordinate in the Russian Bureau and occupies an influential post as Chairman of the Russian Republic's Party-State Control Committee. (Shelepin has the corresponding position for the USSR.)

At the time of Khrushchev's overthrow, Kirilenko had as his associate a second "First Deputy Chairman of the Russian Bureau," Leonid N. Yefremov, whom he outranked, however, since Yefremov was only a candidate to the Presidium. From 1952 to 1958 Yefremov was First Secretary in Khrushchev's home province of Kursk, and evidently earned his confidence. Within the Russian Bureau the men probably divided their responsibilities, Kirilenko being experienced in administering industrial affairs, Yefremov in agricultural; but the political relation between them may be more important than the administrative.

Kirilenko's successor in 1955 as First Secretary in Dnepropetrovsk was Vladimir V. Shcherbitsky, who had been his deputy for over a year. Earlier (1947–1950) Shcherbitsky had worked under Brezhnev in a more subordinate capacity. In February, 1961, Shcherbitsky became head of the Ukrainian government; he was elected a candidate to the Presidium in October, 1961, at the very time Kirilenko was losing that position. Subsequently, however, Shcherbitsky, who is still in his forties, was demoted to his former post as First Secretary in Dnepropetrovsk. In view of his rapid rise and decline, Shcherbitsky's relations with Brezhnev, if known, might reveal something of Brezhnev's influence in his native republic, where he has not held office since 1950.

Despite Brezhnev's prominence in recent years, at the time of Khrushchev's overthrow there were not many top leaders whose careers had conspicuously touched his own. His successor as First Secretary in Moldavia in 1952, Zinovy T. Serdyuk, however, occupied the key post of First Deputy Chairman of the Party Control Committee (the Chairman being the aged and not too effectual Nikolai M. Shvernik). Moreover, Brezhnev's three stints as Secretary of the Central Committee (1952–1953, 1957–1960, and after 1963) were doubtless used by him to advantage in ways that are not clear to the outside observer. For example, on some or all of these occasions he may have supervised the work of three importantly placed figures whom Khrushchev brought into the central Party apparatus from the Ukraine during Stalin's last years, and who held highly sensitive posts when Khrushchev was ousted: Alexei A. Yepishev, head of the main political administration of the armed forces; Nikolai R. Mironov, head of the administrative organs department with responsibilities relating to the armed forces as well as to the political police; [4] and Vladimir Ye. Semichastny, head of the KGB.

A second set of relations center on Podgorny and two key officials who have been associated with him, Vitaly N. Titov and Viktor M. Churaev. Podgorny and Titov are Ukrainians, Churaev a Russian; all were born between 1903 and 1907. These three men in succession governed Kharkov in the Ukraine as Party First Secretary for seventeen years, from 1944 to 1961: Churaev (1944–1950), Podgorny (1950–1953), and Titov (1953–1961). Titov worked in Kharkov throughout these years, first under Churaev, then under Podgorny, finally as First Secretary himself. Thus Titov has had direct links with both Churaev and Podgorny in the Kharkov organization, while the latter two did not work together there. Since 1963, all three have been working in the apparatus of the Central Committee. Until 1953, Churaev was the senior of the three men. He was the first to come to Moscow, entering the apparatus of the Central Committee not long after Khrushchev moved there. Subsequently Churaev was charged with cadre work (personnel appointments for the Russian Republic, then for the Union Republics. Titov moved to Moscow in February, 1961, replacing Churaev as head of the Party organs department for the Union Republics

[4] Mironov worked for a time in the Ukraine as a subordinate to Brezhnev.

when Churaev was promoted to Deputy Chairman of the Russian Bureau. The following year Titov was promoted to Secretary of the Central Committee and Chairman of the Commission on Organization-Party Questions.

Podgorny was the last of the three to arrive in Moscow to work in the Party apparatus. He had moved from Kharkov to Kiev in 1953, when he became a Secretary of the Ukrainian Central Committee, and remained there for a decade before being elevated to a far more powerful position in Moscow than the ones held by the two other former Kharkov Party leaders. His successor as First Secretary in the Ukraine, Pyotr Ye. Shelest, also an ethnic Ukrainian, is probably beholden to Podgorny for his elevation to the position, which in turn led to his being made a candidate member of the Party Presidium. In 1957, the year Podgorny became head of the Party in the Ukraine, Shelest was only a Second Secretary of an oblast committee, although already almost fifty years old. In the next six years he was promoted over more prominent figures, finally becoming Podgorny's successor.

Podgorny's late entry into the central apparatus may make him dependent upon the support of Titov and Churaev, who between them have had a key role for over a decade in assigning personnel throughout the USSR. The formidable appointive authority exercised by the men from Kharkov [5] makes it uncertain how far Brezhnev was able to appoint his partisans to key positions in the Party

[5] A professor from Kharkov University, Yevsei G. Liberman, is the author of the famous Liberman proposals for using market forces to regulate industry, which first received national attention after publication in *Pravda,* September 9, 1962. While there is no direct evidence that the men from Kharkov have patronized him or his ideas, it would be highly significant indeed if it turned out that *apparatchiks* were especially interested in encouraging the use of market forces to regulate the economy.

machine before he succeeded in supplanting Khrushchev as First Secretary. Even after Brezhnev was instructed to concentrate on work in the Central Committee, there was little evidence that he was exercising wide powers of appointment.

What of the abilities of these two leading contenders for the succession, Brezhnev and Podgorny? We have all too little direct evidence about them, although both men, Brezhnev in particular, have been exposed to Western observers. Neither has impressed outsiders as possessing the personal and political qualities needed to rule a country like the USSR. Such judgments are notoriously liable to error. Nevertheless, what indirect evidence is available tends to bear them out. Brezhnev's successful career appears less the product of strong character or preeminent talents than of Khrushchev's patronage, for at each important step in his rise Khrushchev's hand is visible. That Khrushchev thought well of him we know, but not *how* well, nor with what reason.

Podgorny's career is even less indicative of the character and talents of a strong political leader. In the first two decades after his graduation as an engineer, he worked in factories and administrative offices in light industry and, from 1946 to 1950, as the permanent representative of the Ukrainian Council of Ministers at the USSR government.[6] Podgorny was not appointed an oblast First Secretary or a governmental minister, the chief testing grounds of a promising political leader under Stalin, until 1950, when he was forty-seven. Of course, if his slow prog-

[6] This has customarily been a relatively unimportant office. Conceivably Podgorny served in it as Khrushchev's personal representative in Moscow, although Khrushchev did not actually head the Ukrainian Council of Ministers throughout this period.

ress were the result of rivalry or prejudice it would not reflect on his ability, but there is no evidence of this. He had not risen and then fallen, but simply had advanced very slowly—and this in the Ukraine where Khrushchev was boss. While Podgorny's career closely parallels Khrushchev's (see Chapter VI), they have been markedly out of step with respect to age. Khrushchev's began at a relatively advanced age, but once begun it was meteoric: he was only a raion secretary at thirty-six, but he was First Secretary of the Moscow city and oblast committees at forty-one, First Secretary of the Ukrainian Central Committee at forty-three, and a full member of the Presidium when not yet forty-five. Podgorny, on the other hand, at forty-seven had gone only as far as oblast First Secretary.

Whatever Khrushchev came to see in Podgorny after 1950—which finally led to his appointment as an oblast First Secretary, Second Secretary in the Ukraine (1953) and then First Secretary (1957), and finally Secretary of the Central Committee (1963)—evidently had not impressed him much before. As recently as 1960 Khrushchev had occasion to criticize Podgorny for the Ukraine's poor harvest that year, but he praised him the following year for redeeming himself.[7]

Whatever their true ability, the ascendancy of leaders from the Ukraine while Khrushchev ruled assures them a central role in the succession, especially in its first phase, but it does not assure that they will prevail. If they were united in a single bloc, their strength would be truly formidable, but there are important divisions. The chief di-

[7] Khrushchev also directed sharp criticism at Frol Kozlov in 1955, yet raised him to the Presidium two years later. *Pravda*, April 13, 1955.

vision is into the Brezhnev and Podgorny groups, between which Khrushchev had established a balance. Moreover, the ascendancy of men from the Ukraine in the Party machine, both Russians and Russified Ukrainians, presumably has given rise to resentment on the part of others, particularly among Russians who have lived and worked in their native Russia. If there is such resentment, it can only be intensified by the fact that the two top military officials, Marshals Malinovsky and Grechko, are ethnic Ukrainians who have lived and worked in the Ukraine, as is the head of the political police, Vladimir Semichastny. Semichastny, who is only forty, followed Khrushchev from Kiev to Moscow in 1950 as an official in the Komsomol, briefly headed the Party organs department of the Central Committee in 1959, and assumed the post of head of the KGB in November, 1961.

Conceivably—although I know of no evidence for this—ethnic Ukrainians may be at a disadvantage, as compared with ethnic Russians, in any maneuvering carried on by the men from the Ukraine. If so, this might favor Brezhnev and Kirilenko, as against Podgorny and Titov. The ethnic Ukrainians in the higher leadership, it should be emphasized, are completely Russified. They are no less centralizers and opponents of nationalism among Soviet minority groups than were Stalin (a Georgian) and Dzerzhinsky (a Pole), whom Lenin castigated for their "great Russian chauvinism" in the last months of his political career.

The men from the Ukraine constitute a kind of inner circle of those who owe their careers to Khrushchev. There are influential individuals and groups on the periphery of this inner circle, some of whom probably have formed connections with the men from the Ukraine. One of these, Dmitry Polyansky, although he has worked chiefly in Russia, is an ethnic Ukrainian. Polyansky graduated from engineering school in Kharkov, however, and worked there in the Komsomol (1939–1940) at a time when Churaev was already in the apparatus of the Kharkov oblast committee.[8] Polyansky has had wide experience on the provincial level in the Party *apparat,* as head of the government of the Russian Republic, and subsequently as a member of the Soviet government. Khrushchev apparently groomed him by a series of promotions like those Kozlov received before reaching the Secretariat, although with one important exception: while Kozlov entered the Soviet government as a *First* Deputy Chairman of the Council of Ministers, Polyansky was made only a Deputy Chairman. Polyansky's further career may largely depend on the role he played in the overthrow of Khrushchev.

Khrushchev's chief deputy in the government at the time of his ouster was Alexei Kosygin. Like Mikoyan and Podgorny, Kosygin spent his early years in light industry, but he has held major administrative posts since 1940, including that of Chairman of the Council of People's Commissars of the RSFSR (1943–1946). In 1948, when he was forty-four, Kosygin became a full member of Stalin's Politburo, although he was demoted to candidate member of the Party Presidium in 1952 for reasons that are not clear. Kosygin evidently stood apart during the Stalin succession, giving complete support neither to Khrushchev nor to Malenkov, although the latter's faction was generally favored by economic administrators like Kosygin. Even if he

[8] Shelest, Podgorny's successor as First Secretary in the Ukraine, also worked in Kharkov during those years, as a plant engineer.

wished to do the same in the Khrushchev succession, Kosygin was not given the chance, but was made head of the government when Khrushchev was ousted. If the struggle for succession continues for a time, Kosygin might become, perhaps in spite of himself, a leader of the economic bureaucrats in Soviet politics. If Kosygin is a man of ambition, as is quite possible, he may play a major role even in the early stages of the succession.

Anastas Mikoyan, although his relations with Khrushchev were equivocal in the first years after Stalin's death, subsequently made his extensive experience available to Khrushchev as his adviser, idea-man, and trouble-shooter. While he is no less eligible for retirement on grounds of old age than Khrushchev was at the time of his ouster, Mikoyan may prove a valuable adviser to Soviet rulers who are willing to avail themselves of his services. Moreover, as the only distinguished Old Bolshevik still active in politics, he provides a useful link with the Party's revolutionary traditions, and ultimately, if indirectly, with Lenin, the founder.

Mikhail Suslov has had a highly varied career. He worked as an ideologist, in charge of the Agitprop department of the Central Committee and of *Pravda;* as a purge specialist of the Party in the early 1930s and perhaps on a wider scale at the end of World War II, when he was head of the Central Committee's Bureau for Lithuania; as a partisan leader during the war; and as a provincial First Secretary. While he is commonly portrayed in the West as a mere ideologist, he is surely more than this. His role in the purge of Marshal Zhukov has been little publicized, but it may have been substantial. He gave the major report to the Central Committee plenum that purged Zhukov. In it, according to a subsequent account, he emphasized that Zhukov had followed "a line that was leading to dangerous isolation of the armed forces from the Party, that was tending to keep the Central Committee out of decision-making on crucial matters connected with the life of the army and navy." [9] Subsequently, Suslov dealt with foreign Communist states and parties, in Khrushchev's unsuccessful effort to maintain Soviet leadership of a unitary world Communist movement. Suslov's experience in such work goes back almost two decades. He helped Stalin to set up the Cominform in 1947 and then to purge the Yugoslav Communist Party from that body. While Suslov has had the kind of experience that could make him a contender for the succession, he suffers from several handicaps. He apparently has not been able to build up a personal following by means of appointments and has no power structure at his command; he has a tight and forbidding personality; finally, he was ill for a time in 1963 and may be in questionable health. Suslov may play an important role behind the scenes, however, particularly if Brezhnev fails to establish his personal rule.

Gennady Voronov illustrates the unstable position of Khrushchev's favorites while he ruled. He rose to sudden prominence in 1939 as a result of the great purge, being made Second Secretary of the Chita oblast committee at the age of twenty-nine. Thereafter he had a remarkably steady career, as Second Secretary and then First Secretary in Chita from 1939 until 1955. Khrushchev was sufficiently impressed by him on one of his treks into the provinces to

[9] See the speech of Marshal Filipp Golikov to the XXII Party Congress. *XXII S"ezd KPSS* (Moscow, Gospolitizdat, 1962), III, 67.

groom Voronov for better things. He was raised to sudden prominence in 1961 as Khrushchev's deputy in the Russian Bureau of the Central Committee and full member of the Presidium. Subsequently, however, he lost favor, in part because the agricultural panaceas he had advocated turned out badly. Unless Khrushchev's ouster has reversed his fortunes, Voronov's career is on the decline.

Aleksandr Shelepin, born in 1918, is another young protégé of Khrushchev's who has had unusually varied experience for a man his age. He was a Secretary of the Communist Youth Organization for ten years, and its First Secretary for six years. From 1958 until 1961 he headed the KGB, a position which doubtless gave him important experience and useful contacts, but which may also stigmatize him in the eyes of those who fear his continuing influence in that institution. Subsequently, his two-year stint as a Secretary of the Central Committee with responsibility for cadres was a most valuable experience. He remains a Secretary in his current post of head of the Party-State Control Committee, a difficult office which may add to the number of both his partisans and his adversaries, particularly in the economic bureaucracy.

Certain common traits are evident in the men whom Khrushchev has himself raised to high position. Most of them were born in the first decade of the century and entered the Communist Party roughly around 1930. They received an advanced education rather late in life, usually as engineers. Their technical education was relatively good, their education in Marxist thought indifferent, their general education poor. They typically worked in the economy for several years during the first upsurge of enthusiasm for the five-year plan and the more sobering years that followed. The great purge created opportunities for them in the Party apparatus, which was hardest hit, and they entered it on a relatively high level. The great purge of 1937–1938 is something most of them witnessed but did not help carry out; yet it is also true that they did not personally suffer from the purge but rather owed their careers to it. Their participation in the war effort typically occurred outside Moscow, either as political workers in the armed forces—usually in association with Khrushchev on the various fronts where he was active—or as heads of provincial Party organs. After the war they worked in the Party apparatus, typically in the provinces; if they worked in the Ukraine, it was not as members of Khrushchev's staff or as his direct subordinates, but rather as Party bosses in the provinces of the Ukraine.[10] Their careers as *apparatchiks* progressed at a quite moderate pace until Stalin's death or, more often, until Khrushchev's consolidation of his power in 1957. With some exceptions, their age when they finally achieved positions near the top was relatively advanced.

These are the men who, together with a few holdovers from among Stalin's lieutenants, like Mikoyan, were in positions of influence around Khrushchev when he was overthrown in October, 1964. Some were not there yesterday and they may not be there tomorrow. While Khrushchev ruled, men who proved themselves in the provinces were brought to Moscow in responsible posts; those who

[10] A significant exception to this generalization is Alexei Kirichenko, who worked for several years under Khrushchev in the apparatus of the Ukrainian Central Committee, and who was especially favored by Khrushchev in the decade after 1950, only to be discarded in 1960.

failed at the center were thrust back. As a result, there is a considerable group of leaders who have tasted power and gained some experience in its exercise. Many of these men are still in responsible posts; a few, like Kirichenko and Belyayev, were discredited for failing Khrushchev. As a result, a leader or faction in the succession that is able to arrogate power to itself and to purge its rivals may draw upon this reserve of Khrushchev's demoted lieutenants to reconstruct the leadership.

The men who were thrust from power because they opposed Khrushchev are a different case. The seven members of the post-Stalin Presidium whom Khrushchev purged were personally castigated as unfit for leadership. Some of these men, and others who were closely associated with them and suffered a similar fate, were dead or physically incapacitated by the time of the Khrushchev succession. Molotov, who almost alone among living leaders has roots in Lenin's time, could prove useful in establishing the legitimacy of the new leadership, but this is a service he could perform better for conservatives than for reformers. Perhaps only Malenkov (born in 1902), as the original post-Stalin reformer, could actually become a contender for the succession to Khrushchev. Since both Malenkov and Molotov were expelled from the Party,[11] the restoration of either to the leadership would require a disavowal by Khrushchev's former lieutenants of acts they had themselves committed under Khrushchev. In the unlikely event that Malenkov were to reenter the leadership, Saburov, Pervukhin, Shepilov, and others who were associated with him at one time or another, might also be restored to high

[11] Report by M. A. Suslov, February 14, 1964, *Pravda,* April 3, 1964.

position because of their administrative and technical talents, and perhaps because of their reputation as reformers.

PROBLEMS AND ISSUES

These men, or others like them, will be Khrushchev's near-term heirs. They are now faced with a number of serious problems: some are common to all governments in the missile-nuclear era; some are endemic in the Soviet system; still others arose under Khrushchev's rule. These problems, and the issues to which they give rise in the leadership, are unlikely in themselves to weaken the regime seriously or to alter its character radically so long as the leadership is stable, as it was while Khrushchev ruled. During the crisis of succession, however, if it is intense and prolonged, these problems may produce far-reaching effects.

The standard of living. Popular demands for a sharp rise in the standard of living, especially better housing and an improved diet, became a potent repressed force in Stalin's last years. The period of succession and consolidation of Khrushchev's rule (1953–1958) was one of unusually rapid improvement of living standards, both in the cities and the countryside. Since 1958, however, the rate of improvement has been small, and these years have been marked by notable setbacks, such as the sharp rise in meat prices in 1962 and the failure to move toward the abolition of the income tax as promised. This has probably further reduced the credibility of promises emanating from the leadership, and their usefulness in spurring workers to new efforts in production. Unless there is renewed progress in raising standards of consumption, the long-term effects on public morale may be substantial. Khrushchev's heirs face the serious task of devising new measures to raise popular consumption quickly. This task will be more difficult than it was when Stalin's heirs faced it, for they were initially able to make progress simply by concentrating attention and moderate resources on a problem that Stalin had neglected.

Even if the production targets for consumer goods that are established in the Party program were met in the next few years, which is most doubtful, the resulting rise in Soviet living standards, while it would be heartily welcomed, might nevertheless in time create a special kind of discontent. The Soviet people may not willingly receive its increased consumption largely in the form of goods and services provided by the state, as is presently planned, but may demand a greater share of it in the form of purchasing power that leaves them some choice. If such demands are ignored, "material incentives" may fall short of what is required; if they are acceded to, the "psychology of private ownership" may become dangerously widespread.

Related to the general demand for improved living conditions is the people's passion for peace. This already places a certain constraint on Soviet foreign policy; in time it might come to have considerable weight when crucial decisions are made at moments of crisis.

Industrial growth. The spectacular growth of Soviet industry since 1930 has cushioned many acute problems that otherwise might have overwhelmed the Soviet regime. It enabled the nation to arm in the 1930s in order to resist invasion by Nazi Germany, and afterwards made it possible to restore the wealth destroyed in war. During the

Stalin succession the large and growing Soviet industrial base made it possible for his heirs to raise living standards sharply. It provided the means for putting the USSR ahead in the space race and for developing, and in time procuring, strategic forces for the nuclear-missile age.

The period 1958–1964, however, has seen a slowdown of industrial growth. It is not a question of economic stagnation, for the rate of growth remains high. Yet if the slowdown continues, it will increase the pressure on resources, and thereby exacerbate controversy on policy questions that involve allocation of large resources. Foreign policy objectives, particularly those which depend on the relative military balance and on economic aid to underdeveloped areas, may have to be reappraised. Moreover, the capacity of Khrushchev's heirs to cope with the rising expectations of the Soviet population, to give new momentum to the drive to raise living standards, may be seriously strained.

Reform of economic institutions. The slowdown of industrial growth and the failure to make acceptable progress in agriculture since 1958 inevitably have posed the problem of institutional and organizational reform. The question has been debated with relative freedom in the Soviet press, and evidently with substantially greater freedom in unpublished discussion. The most radical solutions entail a large degree of decentralization, down to intermediate governmental agencies or even to production units, and increased reliance on market forces to govern the economy. The solution that is most attractive to the Soviet leaders, however, and the one most resorted to in practice since 1958, has been increased, and presumably more efficient, forms of centralization; but the results obtained, as we have seen, have fallen short of expectations.

The controversy over these alternative types of solution is likely to be intensified during the succession, particularly if growth rates continue to decline. If the result were radical liberal reforms, that is, reforms that reduced the role of the state in the direction of the economy, this would probably further the cause of liberalization generally in the USSR.

Soviet agriculture gives rise to a set of distinct issues. Can domestic agriculture be allowed to stagnate on the new plateau to which Khrushchev raised it in the first years after Stalin's death, or should agricultural investment be greatly increased? If agriculture is to receive much more capital, should it be used chiefly to raise yields or to increase acreage? Alternatively, should the plans for sharply increased agricultural production be abandoned and necessary agricultural products purchased in world markets with Soviet industrial and other products? Would the resulting loss of autarky impair the conduct of foreign policy? Would Soviet cities be able to provide facilities for the requisite influx of population from rural areas? If agricultural production is to be reorganized radically, should the solution be sought in increased socialization, by converting collective farms into state farms in which the workers receive fixed wages instead of a residual share of profits? Or should a radical solution be sought in a partial retreat from collectivism in agriculture? These or similar issues are likely to give rise to serious controversy during the Khrushchev succession.

The technical experts. The very growth in numbers and importance of managerial and scientific personnel that has made possible much of the Soviet Union's economic progress in recent years exacerbated the problem of controlling them. In dealing with this problem, Khrushchev employed coercive measures and inflicted personal hardships on many leading economic administrators. Moreover, he subjected economic administrators to close supervision by the Party machine, a practice that may have been widely resented. At the same time he was able to improve the Party machine's capacity to control the economic process only by bringing technicians into the apparatus. By these means, he succeeded in controlling these groups without employing terror. At the outset of the Khrushchev succession, managers, scientists, and specialists possessed a very considerable political potential, but it remained for them to find a way of actualizing it.

The intellectuals. The pursuit of truth and beauty has always been difficult in the Soviet Union. While Stalin lived, intellectuals were kept in check by rigid controls as well as by terror. In the thaw that followed Stalin's death, large numbers of scholars, writers, artists, and students, though themselves Communists for the most part, intensified their struggle for an easing of censorship over the works of the mind. The regime's response was variable; it alternately loosened and tightened controls, relying now on threats, now on cajolery. The central question remains what it was: can the Party machine reduce its interference in cultural matters sufficiently to satisfy the intellectuals' most persistent demands without endangering its own authority.

The ideological apparatus which enforces the Party's will, while still intact and effective, is probably in need of having its *esprit* restored. It has suffered from Khrushchev's empiricist disregard of the need to preserve the ideology as a coherent whole, as well as his willingness on occasion to overrule the ideological apparatus when directly appealed to by leading intellectuals. De-Stalinization and, in less degree, the subsequent de-Khrushchevization have grossly complicated the problem of controlling the intellectuals by disclosing the dread consequences of abandoning truth as a fundamental principle. It may not be easy to inculcate habits of deceit and intellectual cowardice in a generation of intellectuals who have criticized their elders for having practiced them.

The problem of generations. The generation born in the decade of the 1930s had reverence for Stalin bred into it. When grown to adulthood, however, it was told by Khrushchev that Stalin had been a paranoid monster—albeit a fighter for Communism. De-Stalinization in the spheres of politics, society, and literature, however necessary it was, lacked reason and coherence. It helped to create a chasm between the generation that had to survive under Stalin's tyranny and a generation that knew his reign chiefly from contradictory and confused hearsay.[12] Khrushchev and his propaganda machine decried all talk of conflict between "fathers and sons" if only because the opposition between them had become so patent. Perhaps those of the "sons" who are building careers in the Party machine will not find it difficult to make peace with their elders trained in the Stalin school; but the new generation of educated specialists, if it is able to make its influence felt in politics, could produce far-reaching effects.

[12] See the informal remark by a leading ideologist, F. V. Konstantinov, Director of the Philosophy Institute, to an American social scientist who called for research on children in the USSR whose parents had been victims of the cult of Stalin: "There's no need to talk to children. There's not a single person in this room who has not suffered directly or indirectly from the cult." New York *Times*, June 16, 1963.

The minority nationalities. Almost half the Soviet population is non-Russian, almost one quarter is non-Slav. The repeated purges and persistent charges of "bourgeois nationalism" leveled against Moscow-appointed leaders in the Central Asian, Baltic, and Transcaucasian Republics suggest that these nationalities, or at least their intelligentsias, are still a serious problem for the regime. A strain of national feeling is evident among native Communists in Central Asia and the Caucasus, and in Latvia, at least, among the Baltic peoples. It will tend to grow stronger if there is an extended period of succession. The possibility that political leaders among the minority nationalities may become a disturbing factor in high-level Soviet politics is suggested by Beria's virtually open appeal to these groups to support him against the Russifiers during "the hundred days" of his ascendancy after Stalin died.

The favored position of Russified Ukrainians under Khrushchev makes it seem unlikely at present that nationalist-minded Communists among the non-Slav peoples could hope for support from Ukrainian Communists. This might change, however, if Ukrainians were to be discriminated against once more in the assignment of top positions, as they formerly were under Stalin. Nationality policy may become an issue during the succession, and it is at least conceivable that divisions along national lines might even arise within the leadership.

Weakening of revolutionary will. Marxist-Leninist doctrine no doubt effectively shapes the Soviet leaders' understanding of the political world, but it is not clearly reflected in a strong revolutionary will to extend the Communist system to the countries where it does not yet exist. The Soviet rulers have complained of a lack of ideological fervor in the Soviet people, but some foreign Communist leaders have complained, not without reason, of a comparable fault in the rulers. Their commitment to Communist ideology has, of course, been sufficient to sustain a hostile strategy toward the West; and even if erosion continues, the next decade is not likely to witness a fundamental revision of the ideology as a whole. Yet, living in the shadow of thermonuclear war could subvert particular tenets, like the doctrine that waning imperialism, being desperate and vicious, constantly imperils the "socialist" states. It might also enhance belief in less patently hostile doctrines, even making them the motive force of Soviet policy; thus, the accepted doctrine that laws of social development are bringing all nations to Communism may, in a world threatened by destruction, produce an overriding conviction that this beneficent and inexorable process must not be imperiled by actions that increase the likelihood of thermonuclear war. Attenuation of the ideology, even without actual revision of its principles, could lead to a further weakening of the will to extend Communism, and thus to radical changes in Soviet policies. This process can only be furthered by the great gaps and inconsistencies in Soviet ideology produced by Khrushchev's criticism of Stalinist doctrine, which he failed to replace with a coherent doctrine of his own.

Party hegemony. Embracing all these problems and conditioning their solution is the central question of Soviet politics, one we have already discussed at length: can Party hegemony be maintained, without undue loss of efficiency and popular support, against the impulse toward greater autonomy of institutions and social groups that the Party machine controls?

This brief list of domestic problems suggests how fundamental are the alternatives facing Khrushchev's heirs in internal policy. Now, one consequence of Khrushchev's reliance on rotation in the leadership to secure his power is that his heirs have not been too closely identified with his policies, and therefore feel less obliged to continue them. Stalin had so compelled his lieutenants to praise his person and policies that these policies acquired an inertial movement that had to be slowed down, stopped, and then reversed in a prolonged effort extending over several years following his death. On the other hand, Khrushchev's political personality played so large a part in his style of ruling that his policies will suffer without him to sustain them. Khrushchev's heirs may find his heritage an encumbrance. The economic goals for 1970 established in the Party program, for example, clearly will not be met. If it proves more convenient to abandon than to ignore the program, its faulty construction doubtless will be laid at Khrushchev's door. His heirs will also be tempted to point out the numerous failures of Khrushchev's policies, in order to excuse their own failures. Khrushchev found it expedient to disavow Stalin in order to increase his room for maneuver and his scope for policy-making; for the same reason, his heirs may find it expedient to radically disavow him.

The question of Stalin's reign also seems likely to arise during the Khrushchev succession, although with less urgency than the questions raised by a reexamination of Khrushchev's policies. Stalin can become an issue in two opposite ways: those who regret the passing of the Stalin era may magnify his "services" to Communism in order to mitigate his crimes, which may be palliated and glossed over; on the other hand, liberalizers may intensify Khrushchev's criticism of Stalin. A radically revised estimate of Stalin would probably be associated with criticism of Khrushchev, either for maligning Stalin or for trying to preserve something of Stalin's former fame. Moreover, radical critics on both sides may try to associate Khrushchev with Stalin's actions, the object being, in the one case, to discredit Khrushchev's criticism of Stalin, and, in the other, to explain his failure to be a thoroughgoing anti-Stalinist.

It might be supposed that, while Russia was ripe for reform when Stalin died, Khrushchev has now made the necessary changes in the Soviet system so that reform is no longer an issue. However, the process of reforming a totalitarian dictatorship has no natural term, and Khrushchev's successors are not likely simply to accept what he has done. Probably his tinkering with the system, his turns and twists, have left a considerable residue of dissatisfaction with particular measures. His successors will pick and choose among his reforms according to their personal inclinations. Certainly they will have to decide very early whether to continue pet projects that Khrushchev initiated but had not completed. The overriding question of whether to restore something of what was or to push ahead with more fundamental reforms may prove a highly contentious issue. There is a sense in which Khrushchev's rule was an interregnum which received its character from his leadership, but which his successors may be unwilling or unable to preserve. The Khrushchev succession crisis may be more fluid than that of Stalin, giving rise to greater movement sooner.

Alternatives also confront Khrushchev's heirs outside

the USSR's borders, and are likely to give rise to controversy during the succession. Communist China's bid for leadership of the world Communist movement has not only increased the difficulty of solving long-standing problems, but it has also created numerous new problems that did not exist during the previous succession crisis. The CPR's challenge seems bound to absorb much of the attention and the energy of Khrushchev's heirs. His legacy includes not only the problems stemming from the Sino-Soviet conflict, but also methods of dealing with them that have been too unsuccessful to serve as models for his heirs.

The issue between the two sides is far more than a matter of personalities, yet it centered on the controversy between Khrushchev and Mao. By removing Khrushchev and thus precipitating a Soviet succession crisis before Communist China is compelled to deal with the Mao succession, Khrushchev's heirs have placed the USSR at a considerable disadvantage in the contest for control over the world Communist movement. The CPR may be tempted to intervene in the Khrushchev succession crisis, as it did in the Stalin succession, in an effort to secure an outcome favorable to its own interests. Nevertheless, there will be a pause in the struggle at first, while each side tries to determine the effect of Khrushchev's political demise on the policy of the opponent. Since a basic accommodation on terms acceptable to both sides is unlikely, the struggle may subsequently be renewed, perhaps intensified by Mao's hope of making new gains at the expense of a Soviet leadership that has been weakened by succession. Had Mao left the political scene first, Khrushchev probably would have made a strenuous effort to resolve the dispute with the CPR, perhaps offering Mao's erstwhile lieutenants economic concessions to that end. Perhaps the best chance for an accommodation might have resulted from the coincidence of succession on the two sides. The passing of the two dictators would not have eliminated the grounds of conflict, of course, but it might have predisposed their heirs to make mutual concessions in order to be rid of a quarrel that endangered both sides at a time when they were weakened. If, as appears likely, an accommodation with the CPR will be difficult for Khrushchev's heirs to achieve, they may have to seek new methods of struggle to prevent a further weakening of the Soviet position in the world Communist movement.

Soviet influence in East Europe has been weakened by the Khrushchev succession, probably even more than it was after Stalin's death. When Stalin died, the little Stalins in the satellites continued to look to Moscow, on which they were wholly dependent, for final determination of their policies. Yet within months the order that Stalin had achieved by close direction, police methods, and terror was threatened. Urban riots occurred in Czechoslovakia, where there was a domestic succession crisis; in East Germany intense popular hatred of the Ulbricht regime and a passionate wish to end partition caused a rebellion. There followed relative stability, which lasted until the most acute stage of the Soviet succession crisis was initiated by Khrushchev's secret attack on Stalin. This led to new disturbances in Poland and Hungary, both torn by local succession crises, that endangered Soviet hegemony in East Europe. Resolution of the succession crisis in Moscow with the establishment of Khrushchev's personal dictatorship in 1957 led to stabilization of the satellite regimes in East Europe. For a time, this also made the Soviet position in East

Europe secure. However, the increasing boldness of Mao's challenge to the USSR subsequently resulted in the detachment of Albania from the Soviet sphere of control and its alignment with Peking. The Rumanian leadership availed itself of both the growing Sino-Soviet dispute and the lessening of tension in the Cold War to assert its will against Moscow's on a number of key questions. Partly as a consequence, Khrushchev's plan for integrating the economies of the Communist states in East Europe, which might have provided a delicate but effective form of leverage in these states, has foundered.

Will history repeat itself in the Khrushchev succession crisis, producing disturbances in East Europe followed by stabilization? Or can serious disturbances be prevented? Alternatively, is it possible that the disturbances may be too powerful for Moscow, wracked by a succession crisis, to control? Important elements of the problem of maintaining Soviet hegemony in East Europe will have changed. Whether the new, less harsh methods of controlling these regimes will make Moscow's task easier or harder still remains to be seen; but Red China's challenge to Soviet supremacy in the Communist world unquestionably complicates the problem. If the Communist regimes of East Europe remain stable, and particularly if they win increased support from the people over whom they rule, they may be able to increase their independence from Moscow. Under certain circumstances, they might even be able to exert a significant influence on Soviet politics. On the other hand, if succession crises in the Communist regimes of East Europe coincide with the one in Moscow, the Soviet leaders may be faced with a double problem: to secure these regimes against the disaffection of their peoples, at the same time assuring that their leaders do not oppose their wills to Moscow's.

The point of this enumeration of the problems facing Khrushchev's successors, needless to say, is not to suggest that the regime is near collapse; it is not. The point is rather that these problems and the fundamental issues to which they give rise are likely to provoke serious controversies over policy during the Khrushchev succession. Of course, if the succession is resolved quickly, by a personal ruler's arrogation of power to himself, these problems will become his to decide, although he will not be able to disregard the opinion of his subordinates, of the institutions by which he rules, or of Soviet society at large. If the succession struggle is acute, however, and becomes involved in controversy over fundamental issues, it probably could not be confined within the Party apparatus; struggle over the succession would then become institutional struggle, and the sovereignty of the Party apparatus would be at stake. Regardless of the outcome of such a struggle, its continuation for some time, under the aegis of an unstable oligarchy, would make questionable the Soviet system's evolution along the lines laid down under Khrushchev.

One consequence of an acute and extended Khrushchev succession crisis would be at least a temporary weakening of the Soviet leadership, hence of the USSR as a force in world politics. Whether this would be an unalloyed gain for the West is not the simple question it once appeared to be. The sundering of the Communist world and the acquisition by the United States of strategic forces that can wipe out the Soviet population has led the Soviet leaders to a reappraisal of their overall strategy. The great policy issue of the coming years in the USSR, in grossly simplified terms, may be whether to seek accommodation with the West at the cost of increasing hostility from Communist China and a probable weakening of Soviet influence in the world Communist movement, or whether to press the conflict with the West in conjunction, or in competition, with Communist China, thereby risking thermonuclear war.

IX: Implications for the West

The course and outcome of the Khrushchev succession may have large consequences for the West. The Soviet Union controls almost the only existing weapons that can do great damage to the United States. Our policy of deterrence is meant to influence the Soviet leaders so that they judge it inexpedient to use these weapons militarily against us. Deterrence thus depends in part on the political character of the men who make these judgments. These same men have the power to decide what numbers of such weapons the Soviet economy will produce in the coming decade. Decisions on these vital matters may largely depend on what kind of Communists head the Soviet regime.

Since the issues involved in the Cold War are so great, even relatively small shifts along the spectrum of Soviet politics could be fateful for mankind. Even having a Khrushchev at the head of the Soviet regime, instead of a Mao (or even a Suslov), could have meant the difference between an uneasy and doubtfully peaceful coexistence and a series of military clashes accompanied by a substantial rise in the danger of nuclear war. On the other hand, a Malenkov might have saved the world from such crises as the one that arose in 1962, when the USSR placed strategic missiles in Cuba.

To say this is to dispute the notion that Soviet foreign policy is largely determined by general considerations that do not change with the leadership, such as Soviet ideology (or mentality), the Soviet geopolitical position, and the world balance of forces. On this view, changes in the Soviet leadership are not likely to eventuate in changes of Soviet foreign policy. Such a view seems incompatible, however, with the facts of Soviet history and with inferences from those facts. Had Lenin's active political life not ended in 1923, but continued for another decade until he was sixty-three, it is difficult to suppose that the USSR would be just what it is today. When Stalin died, the USSR was about to test successfully a thermonuclear device and was developing vehicles to deliver such weapons against the United States. The Soviet heavy bomber was publicly flown a year later, and an ICBM was successfully tested roughly four years after Stalin died. Such revolutionary weapon systems, which made the United States vulnerable to direct attack from the USSR, could provide the basis for highly divergent Soviet political strategies. The man who would have made the choice among them, had he lived, had caused the death and imprisonment of millions of Soviet citizens in order to establish "socialism" in the USSR. It is reasonable to suppose that his choice of a strategy would have imposed greater sacrifices, and perhaps greater risks, on mankind than the one Khrushchev actually adopted, and probably diverged even more from the strategy advocated by Malenkov during the months when he headed the Soviet government.

It would be wrong to suppose that leaders of the Soviet Union are like calculating machines that have been programmed according to the principles of Marxism-Leninism, and when given the politico-military facts of the world mechanically prescribe what must be done. If the ruler is succeeded by a man with a markedly different political character (or political style), this has its effect on Soviet policy. But if change in the leadership can lead to change of policy, and if Soviet policy has a crucial bearing on the condition of the world, then it can hardly be questioned that the United States has an important stake in the Khrushchev succession.

The West's stake in the course of Soviet internal development has been widely recognized. Particular strategies advocated for the United States have usually been associated with particular views, or theories, about the nature of the Soviet regime—what it is and what it may become. The advocate of a particular theory is not drawn inevitably to a particular strategy for opposing it; yet each theory has its own tendency, and particular theories have in fact usually been associated with particular strategies.[1] In what follows, an attempt is made to establish the relationship between the respective theories and strategies; to indicate a defect that I believe is common to these theories, and leads to the advocacy of unduly narrow strategies; and to suggest, in very general terms, some implications of the theory of the Soviet regime that is presented in this book for the West's strategy in meeting the Soviet challenge.

Ever since the seriousness of the Soviet challenge was first recognized following World War II, American strategy has been basically a strategy of "containment." A key assumption of containment is that the Soviet regime can-

[1] I have used the term "theory" loosely, to refer to a general view or interpretation, based on reflection, of the character of Soviet politics and its relation to Soviet society.

not be *radically weakened or moderated directly by external action short of war.* In providing its original formulation in 1947, however, George Kennan allowed that *indigenous* forces in Soviet society, or perhaps even within the regime itself, might in time weaken or radically transform it, thereby setting the stage for a possible accommodation with the West.[2]

Kennan argued that Soviet power was but a crust on Soviet society; economic weakness and popular disaffection, aggravated by crisis caused by Stalin's death, would perhaps lead to its mellowing or, what seemed to him more likely, to its radical transformation. What was required of the West was to resist the Soviet aggressive thrust wherever it occurred, while waiting for internal forces to do their work. With the passage of time it appeared that the forces on which Kennan had relied were indeed transforming the Soviet scene, making Soviet rule far milder than it had been under Stalin; yet there was a question as to whether these internal changes had led to any great lessening of the overall Soviet challenge to the West. The new leadership still maintained its allegiance to world revolution, and it even extended the front on which the struggle is waged.[3]

2 There were several variants of the containment strategy in Stalin's last years, however, of which Kennan's is but one.

3 This outcome is not necessarily contrary to Kennan's original conception, for he insisted that only a far-reaching transformation of the USSR would substantially alter its relations with the U.S.: "These, then, are the things for which an American well-wisher may hope from the Russia of the future: that she lift forever the Iron Curtain, that she recognize certain limitations to the internal authority of government, and that she abandon, as ruinous and unworthy, the ancient game of imperialist expansion and oppression. If she is not prepared to do these things, she will hardly be distinguishable from what we have before us today, and to hasten the arrival of such a Russia would not be worth the care or

Recent advocates of the strategy of containment have presented a revised theory that takes account of developments since the Stalin era. On this view, the post-Stalin reforms have actually improved the Soviet capacity to press the contest with the West. Moreover, the West cannot expect future Soviet internal developments to lessen the Soviet threat to U.S. security; their probable effect in the next two decades will be to make the Soviet Union a stronger and more formidable opponent. This view, which has been dominant among American specialists on the Soviet Union, is cogently expressed in a study prepared for the U.S. Senate Committee on Foreign Relations:

> Despite the possibility of crises, domestically and within the orbit, the position of the Soviet leadership promises to remain strong and its commitment to Communist goals unimpaired [so that] a further increase of Soviet power and influence is to be expected. [In] dealing with the Soviet challenge . . . the central focus of our policy should be the political growth and economic improvement of the non-Communist world [since this] course of action [is the] most likely to lead to a modification of Soviet policies in the long run.[4]

The United States is urged to concentrate on containing the outward thrust of what is expected to be a stable and increasingly powerful challenger to our world position.

This theory is contradicted by another that perceives social forces in Soviet society that will moderate the Soviet regime and its policy towards the West. A variant of this theory, which was influential after World War II, held

---

thought of a single American." "America and the Russian Future," in *American Diplomacy, 1900–1950* (Chicago, University of Chicago Press, 1951), pp. 136–37.

[4] U.S. Senate: Committee on Foreign Relations, *United States Foreign Policy: U.S.S.R. and Eastern Europe*, Study No. 11 (February 14, 1960), p. 1.

that as the Soviet regime grew more secure it would become less aggressive and less hostile to the West. This variant and the strategy of appeasement that was based on it were discredited by events in the decade after the war. The theory itself remains viable, however, and it has led some of its present-day partisans to a strategy of supporting and relying upon "liberal" tendencies in the USSR,[5] in the expectation that they would in time lessen the Soviet commitment to world revolution, and the hostility to the West that results from it. (The range of views expressed by exponents of such a strategy is very wide; among them are such diverse writers as Frederick Schuman and Edward Crankshaw.)

Although this theory contradicts the preceding one, they have a key feature in common: both tend to extrapolate the stabilizing post-Stalin reforms into the future. The theory underlying the strategy of encouraging reformist trends, however, asserts that these trends are bound to moderate Soviet policy, a proposition which the advocates of containment deny. The practical difference between the two strategies is by no means insignificant. The one makes containment the dominant objective and would risk impeding liberalization, if necessary, in order to achieve its end; the other makes helping to moderate the Soviet regime the dominant objective, and would willingly inhibit the West's response to particular Soviet pressures, thereby risking particular losses to the USSR, if necessary, in order to achieve its objective.

These two strategies and the theories underlying them have not gone unchallenged. According to still another

[5] Liberal in the sense of "not bound by orthodox tenets or established forms in political philosophy," not necessarily in the sense of democratic.

theory, the Soviet regime and the Soviet empire are fundamentally vulnerable. The West should exploit their vulnerable points by counterpressure aimed at weakening the regime and, if possible, defeating it in the Cold War. This strategy of counterpressure was formally adopted by the Eisenhower Administration, but actual policy for the most part continued to be based on the containment strategy. Secretary Dulles, in accordance with Kennan's original theory, relied on Soviet internal developments to support U.S. foreign policy objectives, especially after serious political disturbances shook the regime in 1956 and 1957; but Dulles made no substantial effort to exploit these developments as a means of weakening the regime. Current advocates of this theory of Soviet vulnerability are mostly on the right wing of American politics and in some circles of the military establishment. In the more radical form in which it is currently propagated, this theory also posits that the Soviet regime is fundamentally evil and therefore is not susceptible to reform or the gradual moderation of its policy.

In my view, the current theories sketched here have a common defect. They present the future Soviet Union that the West will have to deal with as largely determined. The theory of Soviet vulnerability posits a fixed entity which cannot change gradually into something else: dissolution or aggrandizement are the sole alternatives. The other theories project recent trends, as they interpret them, into the future, the one expecting a strengthening of Soviet power, the other counting on the continuing moderation of Soviet policy (so long as the West does not aggravate the Cold War), facilitating a far-reaching accommodation with the West. The strategies derived from these theories are impoverished as a result of the narrow expectations of the theories on which they are based.

In opposition to these theories regarding the Soviet regime is the one outlined in this book, which emphasizes the susceptibility of the Soviet regime to succession crises. It may be called (for brief reference only, and with no pretense of comprehensiveness) "a cyclical theory of Soviet politics": there is a stable phase of personal rule in which it is difficult for the disaffection that exists in Soviet society to gain political expression; an unstable phase of succession crisis, in which dissident groups within the regime have an improved opportunity to influence politics; and a final phase, in which either the crisis is resolved, resulting in some modification of the regime and a new stability, or, what is conceivable but improbable, the dissolution of the Soviet regime.

As judged by the "cyclical theory of Soviet politics," the three alternative strategies that have been advocated seem unable to cope with the range of likely internal Soviet developments; therefore each is defective *in itself.* Yet partisans are inclined to argue that exclusive reliance should be placed on the particular strategy that they favor. Advocates of containment argue against direct action that is aimed at either weakening the Soviet Union or helping to moderate it. They oppose efforts to weaken the Soviet regime as increasing the danger of war, and efforts to moderate it as leading to one-sided and fruitless concessions. Advocates of pursuing victory in the Cold War criticize the strategy of containment as defeatist, and the strategy of accommodation with a reformed Soviet regime as capitulation. Those who wish to aim at moderating the Soviet regime tend to be less restrictive than advocates of the other two strategies.[6] Nevertheless, they view containment as sterile and regard a strategy aimed at victory as bellicose and likely to injure the chances of reform in the USSR. The exclusive claims made for these strategies cannot be allowed, however, since none of them is able to cope with the whole range of likely internal developments.

No particular strategy for the West can be deduced from "the cyclical theory of Soviet politics." However, it implies the need to recognize the variability of the Soviet regime, its capacity for change of character, hence of policy. It points to a broader, more flexible strategy, one that takes account of the various contingencies on which these strategies rely, but does not depend on any one of them. Moreover, the cyclical theory implies the likelihood that the West's policies and actions, particularly at times of crisis—as during the succession—may have a considerable effect on the direction of change.

That the West, and particularly the United States, has substantial means to exert a general influence on the Soviet Union seems beyond question. In today's relatively bipolar world, large decisions by either side affect the political life of the other. When the United States substantially increases its defense budget, as it did in January, 1961, it compels the Soviet leadership to make difficult decisions. Khrushchev's decision to match (in monetary terms) our January increase in military spending, announced by him in August, 1961, had its effect in depriving Soviet agriculture of much-needed additional investment. The USSR was impressionable under Khrushchev.

[6] Advocates of a relatively "pure" strategy of aiding reform in the USSR were influential immediately after World War II, but subsequently were discredited by Soviet aggression in East Europe and Korea.

His overthrow, by unsettling the Soviet leadership and making its course less fixed, has made it far more impressionable. Now, even insubstantial gestures, like state visits, affect the international "atmosphere." The U.S. capacity to affect this atmosphere by granting or withholding such gestures during the period of succession could significantly influence its course. Certainly, substantial moves by the United States during the Khrushchev succession seem bound to affect Soviet policies and may affect Soviet internal development as well. The question is whether the West should try to anticipate these effects and let the anticipation influence its actions.

Admitting that the West substantially affects Soviet internal developments and that these developments may crucially affect the West's future, it may be objected that the West cannot judge the Soviet scene properly and therefore cannot anticipate the particular effects of its own actions. The argument that we cannot judge the Soviet scene proves too much, however: if we are to deal with the Soviet leaders at all, we must make the attempt. When there is a question of a summit conference, for example, it is necessary to ask whether the Soviet representative will have the power to speak for the leadership. (At the Geneva meeting in 1955, Bulganin, the head of the government, lacked this power, as did Marshal Zhukov, and even Khrushchev.) It is but a step from this to ask what effect the summit meeting will have on the Soviet internal situation; not to take this step is a measure less of prudence than of inertia.

The West has a crucial stake in the great questions that face the Soviet rulers, and cannot escape its responsibility for affecting their resolution. In recent years the West (and in particular the United States) has itself become a party to Communist politics. Now a White House luncheon invitation to a Soviet newspaper editor gives rise to a new Albanian polemic against the USSR. Sino-Soviet polemics range on such subjects as "the nature of imperialism," differences in the political character of Eisenhower, Kennedy, and Johnson, how the West will act in specified circumstances, whether the Pentagon is ascendant, and so forth. Of course, we cannot simply act so as to confirm the assertions of the less malevolent Communist leaders. But if we are to play a role in Communist politics willy-nilly, we ought at least to take account of what that role is. Since our power penetrates so far beyond our capacity to measure its effects, we have no choice but to judge these effects as best we can, and to act accordingly. It will hardly do to leave them out of account because we cannot foresee them clearly, which is to place nescience above inadequate knowledge.

When Stalin died, many Western observers believed that his successors were unlikely to fall out among themselves on questions of policy. While recognizing that the Lenin succession crisis had precipitated conflict between Trotsky and Stalin on the future course of the revolution, they argued that the regime's course was set, that questions still unresolved, not being fundamental, were not likely to be a radical source of controversy. Actually, as we have seen, important policy disagreements sundered the leadership during the Stalin succession. Fundamental alternatives surpassing even those of the 1920s now confront the Soviet Union in the mid-1960s. While Khrushchev still ruled, a radical change in Soviet policy, in one direction or the other, was unlikely. With the onset of the Khrushchev succession, the USSR is approaching a new turning point in its development.

Epilogue: The End of Khrushchev's Rule

Khrushchev's surrender of the posts that made him the effective ruler of the Soviet Union, announced on October 15, 1964, came as a surprise to the West, and to Khrushchev as well. The coup d'état prevented him from attending a celebration for Soviet space men he had just announced over radio and television.[1]

Khrushchev's overthrow was the result of a conspiracy, not the culmination of a series of moves aimed at reducing his power. This power and authority, as far as he could tell, were as great in the weeks before his overthrow as they had ever been. Two weeks before the fateful day, a Party Secretary, Ponomarev, hailed Khrushchev as the head of the Central Committee.[2] This acknowledgment of Khrushchev's rule received maximum applause, in which the Party Presidium, seated on the dais with the speaker, doubtless joined.[3]

1 *Pravda,* October 13, 1964.

2 This phrase was part of the Khrushchev cult; by statute, the Central Committee is a collective body and has no head.

3 *Pravda,* September 29, 1964. Of the full Presidium members only Kirilenko was absent.

In August, Khrushchev traveled about the country speaking as freely as ever:

> Some comrades have said to me: Perhaps all these materials should not be published, for you are stating in advance what will be said in [your] report at the plenum of the C.C. [Central Committee]. Why should we make a secret of the fact that the Presidium of the C.C. has decided to convene a plenary session and discuss a report on the deepening of production specialization, on the administration of specialized production? It is all the more irrational to make a secret of the proposal that will be discussed at the plenary session of the C.C. . . . If we do not speak about this now, we will lose much time. For then it would turn out that the plenum would agree with these proposals, would adopt the necessary decision. . . . So I am telling you about this in advance.[4]

Khrushchev's disregard of the Presidium's privacy, his treating proposals as though they were enactments, are testimony to his personal power before his overthrow. At the same time, they suggest why "some comrades" may have resented that power.

Leonid Brezhnev, the heir presumptive, on leaving Berlin for Moscow a few days before the coup, was asked by Ulbricht and his aides to convey fraternal greetings to Comrade N. S. Khrushchev.[5] Their greetings may never have reached the intended recipient, however, for Brezhnev was evidently engaged in a conspiracy by which he would shortly replace Khrushchev as the Party's First Secretary. Whether the counter heir, Podgorny, also played a role in the conspiracy is less clear. A few days before the coup Podgorny conveyed Khrushchev's personal greetings and quoted him at length to a public meeting which chose as its honorary presidium "the Presidium of the Central

[4] *Pravda,* August 10, 1964.
[5] *Pravda,* October 12, 1964.

Committee headed by Comrade N. S. Khrushchev."[6] In the days after Khrushchev's ouster, Podgorny's position in the leadership worsened. Suslov's, on the other hand, improved.

That Khrushchev's ouster was due to a conspiracy and not to politicking against his leadership was further evident in the aftermath. It was announced that Khrushchev's resignation for reasons of health had been accepted by a plenary meeting of the Central Committee, but it is doubtful that the 330-man body could actually have assembled in the few hours available. (Such fictitious plenums are not unknown in Soviet history; for example, the plenums announced in March and April of 1953 may never have taken place.) There was no meeting of the Supreme Soviet to approve the new head of government, Andrei Kosygin, as there had been when Malenkov, Bulganin, and Khrushchev assumed the office. Indeed, because of the strange circumstances of Khrushchev's removal the world Communist movement gave little credence to the pretense that it had taken place in accordance with the Party statute and the constitution. The Communist regimes of East Europe as well as Communist Party leaders in the West quickly demanded of Moscow the reasons for the action, and for the secrecy accompanying it. Provincial leaders in the USSR no doubt were equally eager to learn why the man they had so recently eulogized and emulated had been overthrown.

Why did Khrushchev's opponents resort to a conspiracy to remove him; and how was it possible for such a conspiracy to succeed?

[6] *Pravda,* October 11 and 12, 1964. Sharif Rashidov, a candidate member of the Presidium, quoted Khrushchev in *Pravada Vostoka* on October 11.

A conspiracy was necessary to remove Khrushchev because sovereignty resided in no collective but in Khrushchev's person. Once he had been overthrown, Khrushchev was quickly indicted for having exercised personal rule. *Pravda* criticized "personal decisions" and demanded "undeviating . . . collective leadership"; the Party "came out and comes out against the ideology and practice of the cult of personality." [7] Khrushchev's capacity to maintain his personal power intact despite numerous failures was deprecated by another publication of the Central Committee, which demanded that the leader "experience in himself all the consequences of his errors." [8]

Brezhnev and Suslov each gave striking obeisance to Khrushchev's rule not long before his overthrow. Suslov's obeisance occurred in a major report to the Central Committee at its last meeting before the coup:

> In their struggle against the CPSU and its Leninist course, the Chinese leaders are concentrating their fire primarily against Nikita Sergeyevich Khrushchev. Of course, they cannot fail to see that it is Nikita Sergeyevich himself who stands at the head of these remarkable processes that arose in our Party and country after the XX Congress and that are ensuring the Soviet people's successful progress toward Communism. [*Prolonged applause.*] This is why, for their subversive purposes, they would like to isolate Comrade Khrushchev from the Central Committee and place our Central Committee in opposition to the Party and the Soviet people.
>
> But this foul scheme is adventurist and hopeless, it is doomed to complete and shameful failure. [*Stormy, prolonged applause. All rise.*]
>
> Our Central Committee, headed by that true Leninist Nikita Sergeyevich Khrushchev, is united and monolithic as never before, and the Chinese leaders—and not they alone—should make up their minds to that. [*Prolonged applause.*]

[7] *Pravda,* October 17, 1964.
[8] *Partiinaia Zhizn',* No. 20, 1964.

Comrade N. S. Khrushchev, with his inexhaustible energy, his truly Bolshevist ardor and adherence to principle, is the recognized leader of our Party and people. He expresses the most cherished thoughts and aspirations of the Soviet people. The Leninist line pursued by our Party cannot be divorced from the Central Committee, from Nikita Sergeyevich Khrushchev. This line has raised our country's prestige in the international arena to an unprecedented height, has lifted its authority in the eyes of working people throughout the world. All the Communists and all the people of our country adhere firmly to this Leninist line. [Stormy applause. All rise.] [9]

Brezhnev acknowledged Khrushchev's rule in his eulogy on Khrushchev's seventieth birthday:

The Soviet people will always be thankful to you because, standing at the helm of the Party, you showed courageous initiative in unmasking the cult of Stalin's personality and headed the huge work of eliminating its harmful consequences in various areas of life. The Leninist norms of Party and public life have been restored, the immortal spirit of Lenin has been revived in all its purity and justice. . . .

Standing at the head of the [Central Committee] and the government, you untiringly work for a strengthening of the fraternal friendship of the countries of socialism and the consolidation of Communists of the whole world on a firm Marxist-Leninist basis. . . .

Permit me in the name of all those present sincerely to congratulate you and to wish that in the future also you will serve the great cause of Lenin just as fruitfully, with the same effervescent energy, adding more and more victories in the struggle for the happiness of the people, for peace, for Communism.[10]

Whether Brezhnev and Suslov spoke sincerely or felt compelled to say what they did not believe, their eulogies are eloquent testimony to Khrushchev's ruling position before he was overthrown.

[9] *Pravda,* April 3, 1964.
[10] *Krasnaia Zvezda,* April 18, 1964.

Since Khrushchev's power was so great, how was it possible for the conspiracy to succeed? There were two basic reasons for Khrushchev's downfall. The first is the absence of terror. Stalin was not mad in believing terror necessary to preserve his power against rivals. While it may be that a Soviet leader can rule till the end of his days without employing terror, this still remains to be seen.[11] Khrushchev surely was no innocent, and there is good reason to suppose that the political police was charged with securing his power against any rival. Yet in the absence of terror, some among his lieutenants were emboldened to conspire against him, and they succeeded in neutralizing or winning over the guardians of Khrushchev's power.

Even without political terror, the other means employed by Khrushchev to prevent the formation of hostile groupings might have sufficed, had he not attempted, however cautiously, to arrange his succession. The leading conspirator was the man he had chosen to succeed him. Whether Brezhnev feared the growing power of the counter heir, Podgorny, or was simply impatient to rule, in the absence of terror he and his allies were able to overthrow the ruler and make Brezhnev the First Secretary. But Brezhnev is not yet the ruler, and the succession remains to be resolved.

When the ruler dies, this gives the fact of succession a kind of legitimacy: presumably he was carried off by nature, if not by God. But when the ruler is removed by men, particularly in the manner Khrushchev was, the question naturally arises, by what right was he removed? This question is bound up with the effort of Khrushchev's heirs

[11] Even Lenin, once he fell ill, could not exercise the powers of his office against the resistance of his lieutenants (see Chapter II).

to establish the legitimacy of their rule, and will complicate it. Moreover, if Khrushchev's chief aides did not participate equally in the act of conspiracy, and they probably did not, then this circumstance will exacerbate the struggle for succession. The struggle may be bitter. When Stalin died, the remaining members of the triad he had established, Malenkov and Khrushchev, confronted each other as the chief protagonists. Now the overthrow of Khrushchev probably has brought a confrontation of Brezhnev, Khrushchev's heir presumptive, and Podgorny, the counter heir. It remains to be seen, however, who if anyone will triumph and become Russia's new ruler.

Less than a month before his overthrow, Khrushchev boasted that "the people and the Party entrusted the high post of Chairman of the Council of Ministers of the USSR and First Secretary of the Central Committee of the CPSU to me." [12] But his rule was not founded in the people or the Party. Khrushchev's personal rule finally depended on the institutions of violence, the political police and the army. When the conspirators deprived him of access to these institutions, either by subverting their heads or by physically constraining Khrushchev, his power was at an end. Without the power to command, his authority, which had been sustained by "the cult of personality," dissolved. Khrushchev had arrogated to himself the power which others could seize from him and claim, in their turn, to have received from "the people and the Party." Thus does Russia change its rulers.

[12] *Pravda,* September 20, 1964.

Index

Selected RAND Books

Baum, Warren C. *The French Economy and the State.* Princeton, N.J., Princeton University Press, 1958.

Bergson, Abram, and Hans Heymann, Jr. *Soviet National Income and Product, 1940–48.* New York, Columbia University Press, 1954.

Brodie, Bernard. *Strategy in the Missile Age.* Princeton, N.J., Princeton University Press, 1959.

Buchheim, Robert W., and the Staff of The RAND Corporation. *New Space Handbook: Astronautics and Its Applications.* New York, Vintage Books, A Division of Random House, 1963.

Dinerstein, H. S. *War and the Soviet Union: Nuclear Weapons and the Revolution in Soviet Military and Political Thinking.* New York, Praeger, 1959.

Dinerstein, H. S., and Leon Gouré. *Two Studies in Soviet Controls: Communism and the Russian Peasant; Moscow in Crisis.* Glencoe, Ill., The Free Press, 1955.

Dole, Stephen, and Isaac Asimov. *Planets for Man.* New York, Random House, 1964.

Fainsod, Merle. *Smolensk under Soviet Rule.* Cambridge, Harvard University Press, 1958.

Galenson, Walter. *Labor Productivity in Soviet and American Industry.* New York, Columbia University Press, 1955.

Garthoff, Raymond L. *Soviet Military Doctrine.* Glencoe, Ill., The Free Press, 1953.

George, Alexander L. *Propaganda Analysis: A Study of Inferences Made from Nazi Propaganda in World War II.* Evanston, Ill., Row, Peterson, 1959.

Gouré, Leon. *Civil Defense in the Soviet Union.* Berkeley and Los Angeles, University of California Press, 1962.

Gouré, Leon. *The Siege of Leningrad.* Stanford, Calif., Stanford University Press, 1962.

Halpern, Manfred. *The Politics of Social Change in the Middle East and North Africa.* Princeton, N.J., Princeton University Press, 1963.

Hoeffding, Oleg. *Soviet National Income and Product in 1928.* New York, Columbia University Press, 1954.

Hsieh, Alice L. *Communist China's Strategy in the Nuclear Era.* Englewood Cliffs, N.J., Prentice-Hall, 1962.

Johnstone, William C. *Burma's Foreign Policy: A Study in Neutralism.* Cambridge, Harvard University Press, 1963.

Kecskemeti, Paul. *Strategic Surrender: The Politics of Victory and Defeat.* Stanford, Calif., Stanford University Press, 1958.

Kecskemeti, Paul. *The Unexpected Revolution: Social Forces in the Hungarian Uprising.* Stanford, Calif., Stanford University Press, 1961.

Leites, Nathan. *The Operational Code of the Politburo.* New York, McGraw-Hill, 1951.

Leites, Nathan. *A Study of Bolshevism.* Glencoe, Ill., The Free Press, 1953.

Leites, Nathan, and Elsa Bernaut. *Ritual of Liquidation: The Case of the Moscow Trials.* Glencoe, Ill., The Free Press, 1954.

Rush, Myron. *The Rise of Khrushchev.* Washington, D.C., Public Affairs Press, 1958.

Sokolovskii, V. D. *Soviet Military Strategy.* Translated and annotated by H. S. Dinerstein, L. Gouré, and T. W. Wolfe. Englewood Cliffs, N.J., Prentice-Hall, 1963.

Speier, Hans. *Divided Berlin: The Anatomy of Soviet Political Blackmail.* New York, Praeger, 1961.

Tanham, G. K. *Communist Revolutionary Warfare: The Viet Minh in Indochina.* New York, Praeger, 1961.

Wolfe, Thomas. *Soviet Strategy at the Crossroads.* Cambridge, Harvard University Press, 1964.